This!
The Journey!

A Collection of Poems
By

Henry W. Gurley

This! The Journey!
A Collection of Poems By
Henry W. Gurley

Published by

HEADLIGHT PRESS
6500 Clito Road
Statesboro, Georgia 30461

© 2013 by Henry W. Gurley
ALL RIGHTS RESERVED!

Photos by Fotolia.com. All Rights Reserved!

ISBN: 1-58535-263-2

Other poetry publications by the author:

A Place Called Ace
Neither Fife Nor Drum
Comes Now A Season
Of Time, Of Chance, Of Circumstance

Dedication

This collection of poems is dedicated to two of my most cherished friends: Dean and Carol Lindsey.

To Dean: who has told me he has little patience and lacks compassion, yet with his inestimable forbearance and heartfelt compassion he led me back to Christ. I am humbled by his quiet and steadfast discipleship and honored to be one of his friends. Too, I am honored to call him my favorite duplicate bridge partner.

To Carol: who allows Dean and me to act like rambunctious schoolboys what with our constant but good-natured haranguing of each other's foibles. Carol has a heart full of patience. I am indebted to her for her amity and am proud to call her friend.

Henry W. Gurley
Houston, Texas
2013

Part I: This! His Seasons!

To My Dear Mother

I'll hold sweet memories, I know,
Within my aching heart.
They'll bide with me in ebb and flow
To slowly let her part.

She'll come and go in sweet recall
Of times I spent with her:
Long days in springtime, summer, fall
And winter—then they blur.

My soul bowed to her wise advice.
She beamed with smiles sincere.
Once she called me "sugar and spice."
Such things I shall hold dear.

For as the weeks turn into years
Bright memories will fade;
Then comes the absence of my tears.
Of sternest stuff I'm made.

I'll cherish all my childhood days
Of mother-daughter love.
I'll feel her warmth in golden rays
From Heaven high above.

At last there's softness to my pain
Each time I see her face.
She smiles at me and says so plain:
"I'm in God's special Place."

*(Written for Carol Lindsey in Memory of
Her mother, Marguerite F. Boal. 2/13/18—4/28/13)*

Masterworks

In Autumn when the leaves turn brown
And red and gold, they all fall down
To paint a picture, oh so rare!
I know that God is there

To mastermind His Ebb and Flow,
To stage His wondrous Autumn Show,
To brush His Skies with molten gold.
I watch His Art unfold.

No grander sight could I behold
These leaves of brown and red and gold.
But Winter bodes its icy chills
Upon the snow clad hills.

In time the land, a living scene,
Comes bursting forth in savage green;
And I confront the Season's thieves
That took my Autumn leaves.

But soon a softness in the air!
God paints a picture, oh so rare
Of Autumn leaves that all turn brown
And red and gold as they fall down.

Lightning In A Jar

How quickly they all disappeared—
Those salad days of youth.
The vim, the vigor in my life,
My hapless quest for truth.

Those wondrous days, each gilded in
Thin coats of finest gold;
Sunrises of an artist's brush,
Sunsets with tales untold.

Truly, I lived each moment then
As time raced swiftly by.
I paid no heed to mundane things
And seldom questioned why

That day was day, or night was night;
That stars gleamed from afar;
That what I felt within me then
Was lightning in a jar.

For now the waning ebb and flow
Depict the awful truth:
Those halcyon days have lessened
The essence of my youth.

God's Gift of Morning

At morning when the sun glows soft
    Upon the eastern sky,
  I free myself and float aloft
   Above the clouds so high.

The carmine touch of blazing fire
  Sent forth by God's own hand,
A sight of which I never tire
  Upon the vast, vast land.

His rebirth of each passing day
  A wonder to behold,
And I am awed by colors' play:
  The pink, the blue, the gold.

How thoughtful He in morning's light
  To bring a scene of calm
To all mankind from slumber's night:
  This thing called Nature's balm.

And I am free to go about
  My business of the day,
But first I cannot do without
  This moment when I pray.

My Evening Walk

I take a walk each evening when the sky
Flushes carmine midst shattered streaks of blue.
I gaze in awe at the scene, then ask why
Mortal artists can only look and rue

The scattered splendor as the sun sets low
Far away, far beyond its western reach.
Those selfsame artists sensed the ebb and flow,
Silently quizzed their souls, "What can this teach?"

"Why can this enraptured beauty race on
From eastern environs, then settle in
As if directed by unseen baton?
'Tis for nature to know," they reasoned then.

I take my walk each day at evening's glow
To savor everything they rued. I know.

A Repeat Performance

The primal light of olden suns,
Bedimmed by nature's way,
Erupts again dawn after dark,
Brings forth a dazzling day.

Impassive in its countenance,
Each moment passes by.
No guarantee for tomorrow—
It lights the eastern sky.

With but horizon's arc to guide,
Below, the earth in tow;
From gloom of night to streaking light—
Daily . . . it's nature's show.

Inner Strength

As beauty fades a patina
Comes to emergent view;
Like diamonds after jeweler's dust,
Like morning's sparkling dew;
A face remembered long ago,
Unlined by stress' crease;
Now placid when it's looked upon
In aura of great peace;

Though not surfeit, it has attained
Façade of inner strength;
And in the forward look it takes
Assumes the breadth and length
And width and scope it must regain
To keep an even pace;
And when the sheen of age is there,
It dons a private face.

An Eden Perfect

So still it is; no sounds are heard;
All Nature softly hushed;
Nor leaf, nor limb, nor swaying tree—
My world shall not be rushed;

Nor shall it be disturbed today
For I have need of rest;
This is my choosing, option's nod,
That I shall do my best

To keep it as it seems to be,
An Eden perfect; and
So still and silent and serene—
My world at His command.

If I Could Look

If I could look beyond this place
I wonder what there'd be
Around the curve which seems to fade
Beyond that old gnarled tree;

New worlds which always seem to lure
Attracting probing kind
Could show no more than I have now
With lesser peace of mind;

One thinks the grass is greener there,
Though I may never see
Around the curve which surely goes
Beyond serenity.

Dreamscapes

They never come in ribboned box
    Or on a velvet tray;
Nor do they come upon the eve
    Of special holiday.

They never bow to springtime wish
    Or to the summer's call;
Nor do they heed cool autumn's voice,
    And winter? Not at all.

Upon their silken, silent feet
They walk throughout the night,
And no one sees them, I am sure,
When comes the morning's light.

For in a second they are gone;
    Why do they disappear?
I thought I held them in my heart—
    But were they ever here?

Forever Young

A pity that we all must age
To leave the guise of child
Who views the facets of a life,
Inventive powers wild
To points of sheer absurdity
In blissful, carefree race,
Who shares a moment of great fun
With beaming, impish face.

In time the twists and turns arrive
To urge the child to age—
To step beyond the youthful pose
Of childhood's careless stage.
Quite troublesome that one cannot
Remain forever young
And live full life through childish eyes—
Pray tell, could that be wrong?

I'd Like To Be A Child Again

I'd like to be a child again,
Relive each memory,
And play upon the fields of time
When I was truly free

To romp and race o'er hill and dale,
Or fly a homemade kite,
And stay outside until the moon
Bade the old sun good night.

I'd like to be a child again
And climb an apple tree,
And view the world from that high perch
To see what I could see—

Perhaps a vision of the years—
Or brighter things ahead—
Such pleasant ways of those fine days—
Down many paths they led.

I'd like to be a child again,
For now I've grown quite old—
Though fields of time have been most kind,
My childhood days were gold.

A World Of Sparkling White

When winter in its icy ways
Coats my world in a sparkling white,
I think of August's steamy days
And savor this snowy delight.

The seasons come; the seasons go,
Each one structured by Nature's hand.
A wondrous thing this ebb and flow
Creating beauty on demand.

Along comes Autumn's drying thrust
In colors red and brown and gold:
A time to reap in settled dust
Before the icy days unfold.

Yet, I welcome this world of white,
Awaiting springtime's warming light.

Biding My Time

When I picture April, I see the rain—
Those peppering showers that come and go,
Bringing repair to earthly life again,
Urging long-dormant plants to thrive and grow.

Then comes May in its riotous display:
A kaleidoscope of much-splendored hue,
Forgotten colors in startling array
Softly bejeweled by pearled morning dew.

And I give thanks for these gifts from above,
Far more priceless than the treasures of kings;
These simple gifts of His Eternal Love
I hold close to my heart over all things.

As I await future Aprils and Mays,
I am truly blessed with all the spring days.

Hesitant

I think I'll go and sit awhile
Beneath the old shade tree;
And think on nothing for a spell—
That suits me perfectly;

For neath the comfort of the boughs
The evening slips away;
And for the briefest moment I'll
Savor this time of day;

I hear the calls of nightingales
In plaintive songs of night;
And in the graying distance there:
A hawk in soaring flight!

And hidden in the leaves and grass
The crickets saw their song
In unison of ancient art—
But must it last so long?

And then the darkness settles in;
The night has come too soon;
I think I'll go inside just now—
But look! The rising moon!

And now sheer beauty of the night,
The stars in silvered fire;
I think I'll stay outside awhile—
Or should I soon retire?

As Darkness Rules

The night grows lovely when the sun
Retreats neath western skies,
When shattered pinks and golden glows
Retire as twilight sighs.

And in rare moment comes the night
Against the moon's flat glow,
As darkness rules the forests deep—
But twinkling stars soon show.

And so divine their radiance,
They glint from far away;
And for a spell, the briefest time,
The sun is held at bay.

While far below the creatures of
The ever-changing light
Grow busy in their derring-do—
And lovely grows the night.

In Wondrous Flame

When first I saw a fallen leaf
With hint of autumn's gold,
I scanned the hills and thought, indeed,
What beauty shall unfold;
When at the whim of nature's nod
Within the season's claim,
The world before my very eyes
Shall flare in wondrous flame.

A carmine touch, a citron splash,
A rusty rose, and brown;
And in the mix of palette's hue
The leaves shall all fall down
On city streets, on country lanes,
Near to my cottage door;
Dear God, what beauty You now share;
Next autumn You'll share more!

A Morning's Welcome

A cool this morning in the air
As touch of autumn's balm
Embraces dusty country lanes—
No wind, a chilling calm.
The forest's edge stands silent to
What was a symphony
Of singing birds and chatty squirrels,
Marvelous sounds to me.

And in the fields the trampled stalks
Lie golden on the land;
A dewy glaze on lifeless forms,
Each stripped by farmer's hand.
A cool this morning, and I feel
His Blessings sent my way;
Recalling heat of summer's blasts,
I welcome autumn day.

And I Am Blessed . . .

A butterfly of azure wing
A robin and eternal spring
A nightingale's most plaintive song
A chanting bard of golden tongue
And I am blessed . . .

A dog to bark when strangers come
A bumblebee to drone and hum
A mockingbird to sing all day
An aster for late fall's display
And I am blessed . . .

A child who asks to hold my hand
A cat to purr and make demand
A shady tree at highest noon
A twinkling star, a harvest moon
And I am blessed . . .

An humble cottage on a hill
A fire to thwart old winter's chill
A loving mate, fidelity
His Promise for eternity
And I am blessed.

A Hymnal For September

You don the robe of autumn's light
And pause inside your door;
You view faint mists of reverie;
You cannot ask for more.

Your sunset lengthens, flares from sight
To time of burnished gold;
It steals away for none to see,
Its timeless tale untold.

A sudden hush and all is night,
Yet winds remain bestirred;
You smile with twinge of brevity
At hymns unsung, unheard.

With broadest sweep of universe
You wish September's cease;
You start upon your odyssey
And feel sequestered peace.

But winter bodes with brightness chilled
To skies of ice and white;
You pause to hear your heart's old plea
And rue September's flight!

His Beauty Lives

In May when all the flowers bloom,
When blue skies come to bear,
It is this season I adore;
It is God's Season fair
When in one's heart His Beauty lives,
Tomorrow's hopes abound;
Both in the sun and shadowed glens
His Daily Blessings found.

Indeed, God grants His Beauty that
Makes this—His World—so fair;
Especially in springtime when
His Flowers everywhere
Add to the lushness of the night
And make a gracious day;
In May when grandeur comes alive
In riotous display.

Beyond A Day

A cloudless sky may not foretell
The subtlety of rain;
Nor may a river moving south
Speak twice of arid plain.

A leaf that floats on rippling brook,
Its tree may never clasp;
Nor may a moment poorly spent
Return to selfish grasp.

A snowflake falls from frozen realms,
Reacts to nature's rhyme;
But in a blinding quest of white,
Forever loses time.

And so one's soul in cloudless sky
Shall live beyond a day,
When as a river moving south
It surely wends its way

Unto His Arms, unto His Heart;
Much like the floating leaf
Which finds a snowflake lost in time
And saves from timeless thief.

At Twilight's Glow

It is a touch of Heaven that
I see at close of day,
When in a waning sunset's pall
I note its final ray.

And in rare moment in-between
A change to coming night,
I witness probe of twilight's glow—
Indeed, one special sight!

For then the world comes to a halt;
Sweet rest is on my mind;
And in repose of dreamy sleep,
I leave all cares behind.

It is a touch of Heaven that
I sense at twilight's glow
Though fact that it was made by God
Is all I need to know.

A Rush Of Happiness

Oh there's a rush of happiness
When springtime shows its face
As March and April must appear,
Then May takes rightful place.

The trees alive with singing birds,
The grass a satin green,
Each flower in a striking pose
Complete this vivid scene.

One wonders by what force do these—
The gems of spring appear—
From wintry days of stark and gray
Which started bleak new year.

Oh there's a rush of happiness
As seasons come and go;
And I am blessed beyond belief
To watch His Ebb and Flow.

All Of These

A touch of blue, a touch of gold,
A bit of rainbow I can hold;
A kiss of dew, a threat of rain—
All of these, and I'm home again.

A sandy lane, a field of green,
An orchard that completes the scene;
A stately oak, a newborn fawn—
All of these, and I'm on my own.

A summer breeze, a wintry snow,
And children playing—sleds in tow;
A seashell treasured on a beach—
All of these now within my reach.

A billion stars to glint above,
A promise of God's Gift of Love;
A trust I have unbounded by
His Universe of boundless sky.

In Such A Simple Fact

At morning as the sun comes up
I view a fragile buttercup;
And at that moment near divine
I sense His Presence over mine.

In such a simple fact as this
It is a feeling of pure bliss;
For in a moment—merest span,
I feel His Love accorded man.

And as the sun flames endless sky
It comes to me: The Who, The Why;
And as it dips in blazing set,
I sense His Presence even yet.

As Lullabies Fade

When rain sings rooftop lullabies,
The soft and misty air
Conducts a rhythmic orchestra
That howling winds must share.

From patterned winds the muffled drums
Respond to fury's flow,
Staccato beats in throbbing waves
Rise once and then let go.

This world I love beyond all worlds:
This music of the rain;
But for scant moment I escape—
To be entranced again.

Indeed, God sends a rainbow to
Conclude these lullabies;
In splendored hues an iris arc
Transfigures rain-swept skies.

His Wondrous Worlds

Once in a morning mist I viewed
A world I had not known;
In grace it spread to edge of wood,
In beauty all its own.
In rising till it disappeared
Into a clearing sky,
The mist succumbed as light took hold
In dazzling colors high.

What glory in this small event
Which God had given me,
As wispy traces evanesced
Above the nearest tree.

God daily sends me blessings which
Are worlds of wondrous show;
Without His Hands of artist's touch
So much I could not know.
For through His Gift of morning mist
Which shrouds the nearby green
In filigree encompassing—
His Beauty ever seen.

Far Greater Than

One leaf of grass, one petal of
A rose in fallen fate;
Far greater than designs of man,
Or grand affairs of state.

Perfection's quest that they have stood
And met the test of time;
A lowly sprig, a thorny plant,
In Heaven's thrust they climb

And seek that which we all aspire;
That bright and shiny light;
Far greater than affairs of man—
Much grander be His Light.

A simple sprig, a fallen rose,
Both mortal though they be;
In season's bid they live again—
Reborn like you and me.

Each Striking Day

At dawn His Skies are fused with pinks,
And colors other than
The golds and streaking blues I love;
I know He has a plan.

His Mornings always come at will,
Accepting nature's flow;
They follow darkness of His Nights—
These outbursts I love so.

Oh would His Mornings one by one
Be born in grand array;
And in a throbbing ebb and flow
Be none but striking day.

Though on occasion colors flee,
His Mornings dull and gray;
In timed acceptance prisms bloom,
And brightness comes my way.

Acceptance

The sky spans high and wide today
In cirri-form and lace,
In wispy trails of icy flecks
Which fade without a trace.

The sun looms high and warm today
In gilded glow from space,
In steaming rays of vibrant light
Which darkness must erase.

The sky and sun reach high today
To touch the Master's Face;
And I, below, in humble stance
Indeed, accept my place.

At His Behest

A setting sun turns gold before
The dusk has settled in;
A stretch of blue remains in place
Just as the evening's din
Brings on the music of the night;
When with a carmine blaze
The sun retreats in softened fall
Below the glinting haze.

I know, indeed, that when I see
This scene at end of day,
There bides a purpose to each thing
As part of His Sure Way:
A morning's sun that by God's Will
Shall rise in wondrous show
To set again at His Behest;
This much I trust and know.

Gifts From God

The soulful notes of whippoorwills
And softened calls from fairest hills;
The creaking turns of old windmills;

A golden eagle soaring high
That seems to touch the cirrus sky;
A moon of silver floating by;

An ocean's foam in tidal creep;
In sweet repose a fawn asleep;
And rivers flowing fast and deep;

A misting rain in early May;
A dazzling snow on wintry day;
A rainbow chasing clouds away;

As April comes, a robin sings;
A fledgling tries its fragile wings;
How happy I to note these things:

All gifts from God!

A Moment Granted

How fresh the morning as the sun
    Displays its rising gold!
This is a moment granted that
    I humbly watch unfold.

If every day in sameness came,
    How dull my life would be;
It seems, however, that God brings
    Me vast variety.

With each grand day of grand delights
    I live a wondrous day;
And suddenly, as it must be,
    My time has flown away.

But come the morning and new sun
    Displaying shattered gold,
Again that moment granted me:
    His Grandeur I behold!

It's Lovely When

It's lovely when His Leaves turn dry
As auburn tints in western sky
Give up to night in hued good-bye . . .
It's lovely when His Autumn comes.

His Mornings break in splendored light
And catch the leaves in spiraled flight;
Fall colors all: a bold delight . . .
It's lovely when His Autumn comes.

For in due season leaves are gone,
Tall barren trees bereft, alone,
Shall bud again when suns have shone . . .
It's lovely when His Autumn comes.

His Seasons are His Ebb and Flow,
His Autumns come; His Autumns go,
At His Command comes winter snow . . .
It's lovely when His Seasons change.

How Precious!

How precious are the little ones:
A puppy in distress,
In racing to its master's call,
Rambunctious, makes a mess.

Or kitten with its muffled purr
Which melts a hardened heart;
It snuggles in accepting arms
With dreams a world apart.

Or spotted fawn in leafy glade,
Its mother always near;
It trembles when it hears strange sounds,
Its eyes of liquid fear.

Or cherished tot with beaming smile,
Delight upon its face;
How precious are the little ones—
Each touched by God's Pure Grace.

In A Splendored Moment

Awash in crystal's glow the ice
Defines the early day
Of peeking sun in bluing frame
In pink and gold array;

A million diamonds in the rough
Could hold no greater play
Than that which God in master stroke
Creates with each new day;

For then the brilliance of the sun
Invades the frozen glint,
And in a splendored moment I
May view His Full Intent.

A Morning Mist

A mist enshrouds the treetops in
A film of tattered lace,
And of a sudden reaches out
To cover awkward space;

And as it creeps it seems to add
A softness to its fate;
Then spreads to flowers on the ground
And through a garden gate.

In watered silk—in filigree—
Artistic touch by Him;
Old pathways fade beyond the wood
Unto horizons dim.

And I am gripped in reverie
At this—a morning mist—
And of a sudden I reach out—
An act I can't resist.

A Softness To My World

Comes the evening when shadows soft
Upon my windows play,
I view the world as it slows down
And watch the sun's array

Of colors tinged in red and gold—
And yes! A startling blue
Correct the boldness of the skies
With this, its blended hue.

Odd shadows meld to shades of night,
Infused with moonbeam's touch;
There comes a softness to my heart—
His Gifts are much too much.

Half As Sweet

Though winter's sun is half as sweet
As is the sun of May,
I love its throbbing touch upon
A cold and wintry day.

The blankets of both snow and ice
Perforce must go away;
But I shall cherish most this time
And watch the children play

Upon the hills of sparkling snow—
On sled, on slide, on sleigh—
Their gleeful laughter on the air—
On this sweet winter's day.

Long Ago Autumns

Come Autumn please accuse me of
Embracing lazy ways,
For I shall linger in the woods,
Enjoy the waning rays
Of sunsets burnished twice by gold
Which serve as season's host
To grant a beauty to all things—
These woods I love the most.

The leaves turn brown or red or gold,
Their palettes multi-hued;
And in these dust-filled afternoons
I sense a quietude;
Though in another time or place,
They guarded kindled glow
Among the trees I wandered in—
Those autumns long ago.

Final Destinations

I like the boom of thunder when
It sweeps across the plains
With winds that ruffle settled dust
Before the drenching rain
In sheets like liquid silk they stream
With lightning's jagged blows,
And in assaults of gurgling mud
The creeks and rivers grow

To flow as blood of thickened brown
Where waters once ran clear
And sparkled neath a lustrous day
Before the storms appeared.
I like the peace that always comes
With rainbow's gentle pose;
But standing there I'm wont to ask:
Where does the thunder go?

Heralds

A matter of days, so it seems,
When on a barren tree
Scarred by the bites of winter cold,
A tiny bud I see,
But pay no note that it is spring;
Because the wind blows cold
And I, beside untended fire,
In chill, am hardly bold

To be about my April chores:
To dig, to till, to ply
The musky marbled soil of black;
Though now a buttered sky
With a warming sun offers hints
Of things I should pursue,
For in a matter of few days
I'll bid my hearth adieu.

Do Promise Me

Do promise me that we shall go
Into the woods when first the snow
May dress the trees in capes of white;
No other world, no other sight
Can tug one's heart with such delight
Than this—the best of winter's show—
Above the woods in ebb and glow—
Do promise me that we shall go
Into the woods when first the snow.

April Plus May

When both the sun and roses come
To shine and bloom in May,
I'll dwell upon the fact that I
Had spent one April Day
Beneath a sun whose warming rays
Caressed the greening lands;
And graced the time with plentitude—
Both deeds by God's own hands.

No touch compares to April's kiss
To bring its vast array
Of colors splashed on canvas that
Becomes the face of May;
And when the sun and roses go
To come another day,
I'll thank the Lord that I had lived
One April and one May.

Beginnings

The fog has breathed on windowpanes
To dim my view with mist,
But in the distance trees rise up
As if they must insist
To poke their greening heads above
The softness on the lea,
In brash attempt to find the sun
Which none below can see.

In contrast sharp the world above
Lies blue upon the white
Of puffed-corn clouds in endless tiers;
Indeed, each one in flight
Like actors, who in scripted scenes
Of long-forgotten play,
Recite old lines as if they might
Not ever have their say.

Of sudden break—a probing sun—
Each actor takes a bow;
I wipe the mist from windowpanes
And start my day somehow.

In The Hours Before Sunrise

It's early now; the eastern skies are dark
Where only yesterday a thrusting gold
Had nudged metallic disk above the trees
And added pinks and scarlets to its face
As hours unfold.

It's early now; there are no warbling trills
Of night birds' plaintive songs upon the air,
For they have gone to secret nesting place
To bide their time 'til one more setting sun.

It's early now; though dimmest light is seen
Through black, through gray, through filaments of blue,
The breeze is calmed until the sunrise bolts
And splatters golden blood upon the skies
As nighttime dies
Before sunrise.

In This Peaceful Time

At sunset when the shadows come
To mask the edge of night,
I revel in this peaceful time
As darkness swallows light

In softness that infringes on
The starkness of the day
To bring the thrust of torrid sun
To shadowy display;

And stir the breezes to new life
In fragrance subtly sweet;
Then bid the creatures of the night
Their dulcet songs repeat

At sunset when the shadows fall;
My tensions fade away;
And at this time I'm happier
Than I have been all day.

My Littlest Friends

Who'll see to them when I am gone,
Tend to their daily needs?
Who'll fill the bird baths twice each day?
Who'll buy sunflower seeds?

Who'll watch them hop about to choose
The morsels they shall eat?
Who'll watch them seek the cooling shade
Before the mid-day heat?

In twilight's calm, when they return
Before the night descends,
Can I be sure that they are loved—
These ones—my littlest friends?

I should not worry, for they are
Forever in God's care;
And I'm assured He'll see to them—
My littlest friends out there.

A Whimsy In Blue

I long to see the color of
The blue at mid-day when
The clouds have stretched like billowed sails
To start their journey; then

Have moved to other kingdoms where
The skies may not be blue,
Or where there is no ocean breeze,
Or mid-days overdue.

I long to see the color when
The blue returns to me
Behind the puff of billowed sails—
No grander sight you'll see.

I wonder what would happen if
The clouds should go away
To leave me with a somber noon
Against a sky of gray;

But even then I'd long to see
The blue that I love so,
Stretch out too far, too wide, too deep,
To regions it dare go.

At Autumn's Door

I long for cooling autumn winds
That swirl in dusty chase
Of scattered leaves of lustrous hues
That tumble place to place.

A hint, perhaps, of things to come
On cool October day;
When leaves are blown about like chaff
To slowly find their way

To autumn's door at garden's gate
In peace and quietude;
And I'll be happy for a spell
In this, my solitude.

A Slice Of Life

How fragile they, the little birds,
That beg for morning seed
And fluff their feathers, shake their wings—
True Nature's sight, indeed.

And all a-quiver they demand
Attention over all
As feed or tasty morsel comes
With every chirping call.

But in due time the chirping ends,
And to a tree they fly—
Mere fragment of a slice of life
That touches me—but why?

A Starring Role

The moon glows full, a golden plate
 Against the flattened skies;
So still and mute it inches through,
 To other region plies
Where in an instant subtle change
 To one I view just now;
Remakes itself to gleam again
 With shining face somehow;

Mere harbinger of day to come—
 When lemon orbs may be;
I thought the moon, a sun long-dead,
 Could never come to me;
But high above it taunts the sun;
 It flaunts its silver face,
And bides its time for entrance when
 It takes its destined place.

Each Day A Gift

He'll never know the flush of fame
Or commendations' roars,
Or sense the power of elites
Who saunter through front doors.

He'll never hear fine crystal's ping
Or clash of silverware,
Or feel the crisp of linen's kiss
Or sit in gilded chair.

He'll never warm to cozy stove
Or honeyed cup of tea,
Or proffer toasts to sailing ships
As they put out to sea.

He'll never meet a pretty lass
Who gives him second look;
His pockets empty as his heart,
His life an open book.

He bides his time on windblown street
Before his jig is up;
And knows each day is still God's gift
Which more than fills his cup.

Good Neighbors

Lifeless, the molten moons have shown
What burning stars once told:
Demise of a thousand suns, gone
To vacuums draped in cold.

Once though an animus, a spark
Breathed life: a fiery red;
Enlightened gray gloom and deep dark
Of galaxies now dead.

They circle; they circle and spin;
These silent catalogs
Of unnamed rocks without, within,
Lost in galactic fogs.

Little Boys, Little Men

Summer! Summer! The season when
    Little boys become little men;
And build their forts in shady trees,
And sail their ships on pirates' seas;
    And storm imagined citadels,
    And rout the faithless infidels.

But come the fall when schools begin,
    The little boys no longer men;
    No forts to man in shady trees,
    No ships to sail on pirates' seas;
    No storming lofty citadels,
    No routing faithless infidels.

    It's back to school and ABCs;
No forts, no ships, no pirates' seas;
    Citadels? None! No infidels;
It's back to books and ringing bells.

Summer! Summer! The reason then
    Boys grow up as stalwart men;
But stalwart men seek childhood joys
And change from men to little boys . . .

Dream Trips

I may have gone to other worlds
In another age
And regaled all with fabled tales
From a golden page.

I may have flown by streaking stars
On a feathered wing
And slipped into a rainbow, and
Heard an angel sing.

I may have dreamt the dream of dreams
Through the longest nights
And scattered dust of galaxies
On my starry flights.

But home am I, and home I'll be
For a night or two;
And then my dreams will spirit me
Far beyond the blue.

Let Me Be

Place a flower on my grave;
I was but an humble knave.
So let me be; let me be.

Plant a rosebush where I lie;
May it bloom to kiss the sky
And see to me; let me be.

A fraction once, now I'm whole,
Basking in my new-found role.
Don't add to me; let me be.

Brief this term of sweet repose;
Thus it ends; and thus it goes.
At least I'm free; let me be.

If the sun should cease to rise,
I'll not know, too blind my eyes.
I'll never see; let me be.

Laugh a bit; or shed a tear;
Be not dismayed; I am here.
Do these things; then let me be.

Missing Autumn

I miss the Autumn when it's gone;
I miss the swirling leaves—
The crimson ones, the golden ones—
For these my heart now grieves;

I miss the mornings when the dew
Is pearled with dusty touch;
And looks like breath upon a glass—
Oh this I miss so much!

I miss the smoking, burning leaves
There is no other smell;
I miss the pumpkins brightly orange—
And cornstalks shocked as well;

I miss the church bells ringing out
Upon the village square—
A hymnal for reflection and
I miss not being there;

I miss those days so long ago
When nature made its call
To bring the season I adored—
God's Season I called Fall.

As My Friend

I know He hears me whispering
When comes a sudden breeze;
Or when the wind goes rushing through
The boughs of gnarled old trees;

I know He hears my anxious voice
When comes a stormy day;
In thunder's boom, in roaring gusts,
In lightning's sharp display;

I know He hears my praise to Him
When comes His rainbow hues;
And in the early morning when
I welcome crystal dews;

He hears my whisper on a breeze,
My voice upon the wind;
He shares His rainbow's bright array—
Then listens . . . as my friend.

Death At Sunrise

An early mist in flimsy veil
Deflects the waning night
To mask its separation from
Intrusive morning light;

But gone as if in seconds that
Were never meant to be
To then return at new day's break
To blanket grand old tree

In mystic shroud of liquid lace
Resplendent to the eye
Short-lived this fragile dewy garb—
At sunrise, it must die.

A Time Of Sweet Retreat

Just down the road around a bend
A quiet place I know,
Where on a meadow splashed in green
Such lovely flowers grow.

At forest's edge the violets
In gracious hints of blue
Put forth their faces timidly;
Expressions: "What to do?"

And there beneath an ancient oak
Stand lilies bathed in light;
And oh, the presence they command—
Indeed, a golden sight!

I know these flowers offer me
A time of sweet retreat,
Providing me a comfort that
Can make me feel complete.

And when I go just down the road
To linger in this place,
I know full well what I shall find:
The essence of God's Grace.

A Place I Cherish

I know a place where I can dare
To dream my dreams in peace,
Forget my troubles and then share
A blessing's sweet release.

A tiny stream in gurgling flow
Invites me to this place,
And as I follow it I know
The essence of His Grace.

Each flower peeks in beauty's pose
Near to a dappled glade;
I linger there to touch a rose,
A wonder He has made.

This place I cherish as I dwell
In boundless reverie;
And for a moment all is well
Within the heart of me.

In Awe Of What I See

A river flows to points unknown
On which a lifeless moon has shone.
I think upon my bygone days
And rue the errors of my ways.

An ocean in a raging storm,
A melting sun to keep me warm;
I sense a flow within, without—
A feeling there I cannot doubt.

A little stream goes rippling by,
And high above how blue the sky.
I stand in awe of what I see:
Reflection of His Majesty.

My pulsing heart in rhythm to
The little stream, the skies of blue;
And He in all His Majesty
Somehow has time to care for me.

It's Winter Now

The snow now drifting, piling high
Against the fences, and the sky
Runs brightly clear to endless climes.
It's winter now, the best of times.

The rabbits traipse upon the snow:
I wonder if they dare to know
All regions of this dazzling land.
I wonder if they understand
This season when the snow piles high,
The azure of the sun-kissed sky,
Or whether they by fate's decree
Accept this time like you and me.

The trees like sentinels in white
Against the forests, and the light
Grows dim and fused to farthest hill.
It's winter now until, until . . .

Encore At Twilight

As dusk draws near a peace evolves,
Adds closure to the day
And in this pageant softened hues
Upon the shadows play.
But oh, the music when the night
Upon the twilight floats;
It is a world of symphonies
That strike discordant notes.

Where were these sounds at highest noon
When brightness ruled the day?
Musicians all at eventide—
But who held them at bay?
Again the softness of the night—
Again the music's score—
Anew the purpled majesty!
Applause! Applause for more!

And I Remember

It's wintertime, and oh the ice!
Its crystals and its diamonds splice
The view against a rising sun
As prisms glint and colors run.

Not long ago when all was green,
I could not dream of such a scene.
The heat embraced by heavy air—
I wished back then for autumn fair.

And soon, quite soon, September's hold
With slowing days of melting gold;
And I remember times ago
When I awoke and saw first snow.

It's wondrous that each season must
In special ways convey one's trust:
That in the course of each good thing
God soon shall bid a robin sing

To herald grandeur of spring day;
Then summer shall in His sure way
Bow low to autumn's burnished clime—
And oh, shall come His wintertime!

Learning To Pause

My day begins, and I am slow
On purpose, I suppose;
I yearn to savor everything
On which my spirit grows.

A bursting sun, the fogdraped trees,
A veil of misty air;
A rose that wakes from dewy trance
On this a new day rare.

Odd though it be that each day comes
With promise of fresh start,
The glowing of each sunrise seems
To warm my aging heart.

And so it is that I begin
With purpose, I suppose;
I've learned to stop, a moment's pause—
Take time to smell a rose.

A Morning Evanescent

It is the time when I grow calm
In peaceful quietude;
To stand before the coming night
In grip of solitude,

And think on things which bring great peace
To body, heart and soul;
To thus consider how He has
Made me complete and whole;

Without a doubt I have attained
The mantle of repose
To greet the advent of the night
And bid my day to close;

The hours to come shall bring my rest;
And I shall rise to see
A morning evanescent in
The peace that He brings me.

God Must Will It So

Shadows fall at twilight; misty haze draws near;
Golden sun now melting; twinkling stars appear.
Azure skies grow stellar; depth without a sound;
Hush of night inviting; mysteries abound.
Silver moonlight plated 'gainst an endless sky;
Children staring skyward asking "Why? Oh why?";
Silence salved like ointment ending weary day;
Streaking comets speeding past the Milky Way.
In a fleeting moment worlds may fall asleep;
Others shall awaken from their slumbers deep;
Universe performing; God must will it so;
Shadow's flee at daybreak at His Morning's Glow.

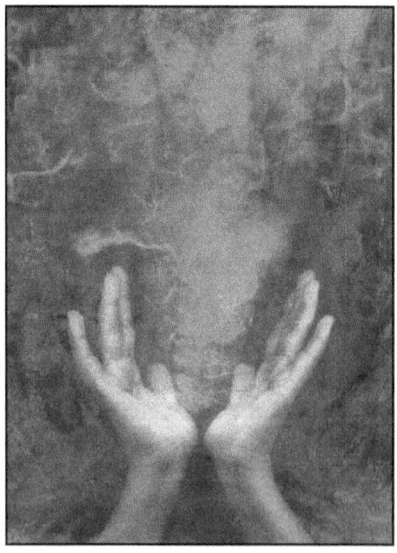

For, Lo, The Winter Is Past

For, Lo, the winter is now past,
The rains are over; and
The trees' new green is towering
Above the glowing land.

All creatures warm themselves unto
A rising orb of gold
Which once looked down on dazzling white,
A world distressed by cold.

But near a growth where brambles stretch,
Is that an early rose
Beneath old sweep of graceful winds
Where banked the wintry snows?

An aura here: of Faith and Hope
In blended gold and green;
For, Lo the winter is long past—
Indeed, His wondrous scene!

*Song of Solomon 2-11

As Skies Bend Near

The skies bend nearer to the earth
As days grow shorter still;
And in a golden glow afar
A sudden autumn chill;
And black and gray and slate appear
As harbingers of night;
Intrusive to a summer day
Perforce to make its flight.

Beneath a newer, vibrant sun
A summer, though less bold,
Extends itself and fades to dim
As autumn takes its hold.
In glory days of melting suns
October hints of chill;
And now, indeed, I think I see
The thrust of nature's will.

As skies bend nearer to the land
Acceding as they must,
Accepting autumn's placid ways
In golden rays of dust.

A Bird Upon The Wing

What glory in the music of
A bird upon the wing!
Within its paradise of life
Its songs so sweetly ring.

Upon an edge of morning's break
Sharp trills float on the air;
And in the din of busyness
Its notes sound everywhere.

Would that I be a maestro of
Such instrument of song!
Upon my stage in lavish praise
I'd sing the whole day long.

But I shall leave the singing to
A bird upon the wing;
Its arias of wondrous scope—
Full measure they shall bring!

Awaiting Morning's Glow

Too soft the evening in a hush
In purple mists of night;
In hazy tint to fading day,
As moon of silvered light
Looks on the scene, broad face aglow,
And drifts against the sky;
Below, the world, in darkened crawl,
Withdrawing by the by.

And night holds on in timeless hedge
To test the morning's glow;
When of the calendar's decree
A world's awakened flow
Announces break of harsher light,
Infused to streaking day,
When reds and golds and strident blues
Upon a morning play.

A Frost Glints Silver

A frost glints silver on the lawn
From moonlight high above;
A bracing night of sheer delight,
It is a time I love.
And should I dare to leave my hearth,
I'd view an endless sky
Of starless night with silvered light,
Then shiver by the by.

But morning breaks with warming rays
In golden tone of day;
In comfort's chair I tarry there;
The frost anon at bay.
But it shall come again, I'm sure,
With sunset's fading glow;
A chilly night in autumn's light—
Perhaps a trace of snow.

Beholden To The Golden Leaves

Bright, golden leaves are all I need
To start my autumn days;
Along the paths they lie in state
In season's grand displays;
But soon they're joined by reds and browns,
First scattered by faint breeze;
Then swirled by winds of hazy dawns
Which rustle through the trees.

November hints of dusty cool
As leaves blend lifelessly—
Mosaic of a hued demise
Which greets eternity.
December bids when come the snows
To blanket all scenes white;
I watch with sadness as the leaves
Are taken from my sight.

But I Shall Think Of Winter

I'll think of winter when the snow
In patterns lacy white
Begins to fall on chilly eve,
Continues through the night;
And when the morning sun shall break,
My view: resplendent sight—
A realm aglitter; oh, the glow!
My fancy takes its flight.

In time comes due the beauty of
Each season that one knows:
Lush velvet green of springtime and
A brilliant summer rose;
But I shall think of winter when,
Released from autumn's throes,
My graceful world grows whitely hushed
Beneath the fallen snows.

As Seasons Come My Way

As little bit of happiness
A lilting song to sing
An April sun on springtime run
May flowers it should bring
And then the heat of summer comes
To wilt the greening land
The August days with scorching rays
Too much one cannot stand

Erelong the brush of autumn's hue
When coolness fills the air
The golden touch I love so much
It comes with subtle flair
But then the winter blustering
With winds of bitter cold
A gripping vise of snow and ice
A whiteness must unfold

Grant me a bit of happiness
As seasons come my way
Of hopeful time in special clime
To bring another day.

I'm Thankful

In the thin, blue veil of morning,
Or twilight's rose and gray,
I'm thankful for so many things
That He has sent my way:
The great, dark oaks in forests deep—
Faint smoke in idle rise—
The gurgling talk of rippling creeks—
A crystal dew's surprise.

A rainbow's arc at eventide
When rain has disappeared;
The foiling black of storm clouds that
I've both admired and feared.
Enchanted evenings as the dusk
Enraptures and endears
Me to the places that I love
As nighttime gently nears.

I'm thankful for so many things
That He has sent my way
Within His veil of morning and
His rosy close of day.

In His Way

His Beauty's in a rainbow and
A sunset's fading glow;
And on the farthest white-draped hills
Where dazzling lies the snow.
On stormy seas the raging winds,
Destructively complete,
Bring music to the salty air—
So brutal, but so sweet.

And there! A dulling thunder from
The silent, endless plains;
One savors liquid treasures of
Full onslaught of His Rains.
Comes April when the fragile blooms
Sway rhythmic to the breeze,
One thinks of chilling days ago
And winter's savage freeze.

God sends His Beauty in His Way:
The sunsets, dazzling snows,
The raging seas, and soaking rains,
And April's spring-like shows.

In A Golden Silence

When in a golden silence, I
   Consider all good things;
I find a moment precious to
   The happiness it brings.

Consider: singing birds at dawn;
   Consider: shady trees;
Consider: kites afloat in March
   Upon a sudden breeze.

The list goes on, and on, and on:
   A never-ending praise—
When in a golden silence, I
   Think on these happy days.
Old sages tell us, as they should,
   Reflective souls grow glad,
Bound by a moment precious to
   Reflections each has had.

So I, in golden silence, shall
   Consider all good things;
And praise my God, as well should I,
   For blessings that He brings.

At Morning When . . .

At morning when the world grows soft,
The trees in foggy screen,
And flowers nodding, half-asleep,
A perfect Eden's scene
Which in a moment as the sun
Sends out a probing ray;
In clarity of golden blend
Creates His Promised Day.

It is a time that I await
To seek His Healing Balm;
And in departure of the night,
My soul finds morning's calm;
For then my world is full, alive;
The green accenting trees;
And flowers swaying vibrantly,
Accepting freshened breeze.

And all is well, as it sould be;
My world in His Control
At morning when the world grows soft—
My spirit is made whole.

His Miracle Of Autumn

I'll take a walk along a trail
When first bodes autumn's chill;
I'll revel in the fallen leaves
Until I've had my fill

Of reds and golds and parchment browns,
Their colors near-divine;
I'll sense, indeed, the Master's touch—
This beauty His, not mine.

I'll thank Him for this season when
The leaves turn golden, and
When reds and browns fall lazily
Upon His drying land

To paint His picture year by year
In scenes I shan't forget—
In splendor of His autumn that
Has never failed me yet.

If Such A Day Permits

If such a day permits me to,
I think that I shall go
Outside where I can stir about
And watch the springtime show
Of children who've discovered in
The branches of a tree
A woven nest with speckled eggs—
No grander sight indeed.

Or view a fawn in no distress,
Its eyes so tenderly
Reacting to the new-found sounds
Beneath a shady tree;
Or gaze in awe as farmers plow
Brown ribbons laced in green
And hear commands of "Gee!" and "Haw!"
On this the April scene.

If such a day permits me to,
I think that I shall go
Outside where I can stir about,
But not today – it's snow!

Dancing Sunbeams

If sunbeams dance on autumn leaves,
If colors flare in light—
If shadows move with random ease
Then disappear from sight

To come again as if perforce
As partners in a dance—
If leaves of brown and red and gold
Must miss autumnal chance

To boast full shadings for kind eye
Of suitors of the fall—
If dry and dusty winds of fate
Bid autumn make its call

Then one more day of dappled light
Upon a fallen leaf—
September goes; October comes—
Perverse this sudden thief;

If in a chilling moment when
The skies turn ashen gray—
If sunbeams dance on falling leaves—
Then summer's gone away.

It's Springtime!

How soon they come when first the spring
    Bursts forth in green surprise
To fill the glades with April's touch—
    Awaken wintry eyes;

I watch them swoop and soar, and float
    In busy, festive flight;
And hear their songs from budding trees
    At morning; then at night

When other members of their choir
    Hit notes on plaintive scale;
As April eves prepare for May—
    It's springtime, I can tell!

If I Should Hear A Songbird

I'm thankful for the simple things,
    The songbirds most of all
That bring me pleasure in the spring
    With vibrant, trilling call;

And in the heat of summer when
    The lazy days appear,
I hear the chipping sparrows and
    Their notes of charm and cheer;

And when the golden crisp of fall
    Brings dusts of quietude,
I listen for the plaintive doves
    And sense a solitude;

For then the graceful sweep of snow
    Flaunts winter's chilling white;
And should I see a purple finch,
    Its warbling brings delight;

And once again in early spring
    Come robins to announce:
"Cheer-up, cherrily; tut-tut-tut!"
    They give my steps a bounce.

First Snow

It is a time that I love so
When comes the first of season's snow;
And down a country lane I go
In winter's sheer delight;

The holly leaves in beauty's pose
With berries redder than a rose—
And is that frost that tweaks my nose
As sunset bows to night?

I see some tracks – were rabbits here? –
For in the brush they disappear;
I wonder if they left in fear
To burrows out of sight;

It is this time which brings me cheer,
A season that I cherish dear;
A special fragment of my year—
I love this world of white!

A Matter Of Preference

When winter comes, there may be snow
And biting winds of cold;
And on some mornings there may rise
A sun of frozen gold.

Its light may scatter crystal glint
Upon the white-hushed snow,
Like diamonds in a sparkling stream
Where clear the waters flow.

Though on a morning when the skies
Grow blighted with dulled gray,
No frozen gold, no crystal glint
But cold – a wintry day.

Each winter brings its beauty that's
As lovely I would guess
As spring, or summer or the fall—
Though I prefer it less.

How Lovely Now

How blue the skies ! Though twigs are strewn
    And leaves lie here and there;
  At edge of wood a shattered oak,
    Its roots grasp empty air;

And in near distance fallen limbs
    Exposed as rudest sight
Where fields once stretched in symmetry,
    Now ugly in full light;

  Where roamed the cattle on a lea
    By streams of crystal flow,
  Now roiling with a muddy rage,
    In labored movement go.

In time old wounds shall heal themselves
    With nature's placid grace;
  And storms forgotten, set aside—
    How lovely now this place.

Morning: All Is Well

The fog has lifted, and the trees
Resplendent in their changing green
Now face the sun; a morning breeze
Adds movement to this early scene.

Beyond the hills a golden glow
Enhances scattered pink and blue;
And crimson streaks from far below
As sunbeams glisten on the dew.

And all is well, as it should be:
Unfolding of God's world each day;
I take a moment knowing He
Has made the sun to light my way.

A Country Lane

A country lane on a summer day
And in the sunlight shadows play
And dart ahead to babbling brook,
Inviting me to stop and look.

They bid me tarry in the glade
Near the water in cooling shade
Where I may view God's skies of blue,
Consider options: what to do.

At edge of wood stands watchful deer,
A nervous twitch as I draw near;
Of a sudden it runs away—
Will it return another day?

And up ahead a meadow which
Saw lands once tilled, the soil so rich;
Now covered with neglected green,
But even yet a lovely scene.

A country lane on a summer day . . .
And in the sunlight shadows play . . .
And dart ahead to lead the way,
Inviting me to stop – and stay.

It's wintertime! The country lanes!
One wonders where they go.
I think today I'll bundle up
And take a walk. I'll know!

Beyond A Moment's Pause

Across the weightless time of years
   Like clouds before the winds,
In fear and compromise a ghost
   Bereft, no message sends

From driven days and turgid nights,
   Beyond a moment's pause;
Or in an echo's voice repeats
   "Because! Because! Because!"

Not on its roof would drumming rain,
   With taut discretion's care,
Exhort the winds to hie away
   With numbing, drumming flare.

It hastens forth to chalky end,
   This specter of the night;
And spans the years in whitened rage,
   Accedes with stubborn fight.

It's over . . . it has come to pass;
   Small questions left behind;
The lovely segments of ago . . .
   Each blends to spectral mind.

A Dream Of Winter

I've dreamt of winters long ago
When on the trees the fallen snow
Appeared as puffs of cotton white;
And rabbits burrowed out of sight;
And redbirds in their jaunty red
Flew hither-thither o'er my head,
Then sought prized morsel in the snow;
A childhood winter long ago.

And sleigh bells rang down country lanes;
Crisp snowflakes etched my windowpanes;
Secure at home with fires aglow;
A childhood winter long ago.
October's gold, November's rain
Now offer promise once again
To bring the season I love so:
December with its welcome snow.

And I stay home by hearth and know
The secret tinge, that heartfelt glow;
My windows frame this world of white
In childhood's dream on winter's night.

A Kingdom Of My Own

Upon a sparkling wintry morn
As snow in graceful flight
Designs its flakes in lacy weave,
And all my world turns white,
I rise to greet the wonders of
This season now full-blown;
And find a realm of fantasy,
A kingdom of my own.

My cottage all aglitter, and
My forests twice aglow;
My lamp shines golden in my room;
I seek no place to go.
Upon a sparkling wintry morn
My thoughts, my dreams conspire;
Outside the snowflakes lacy white—
Inside a warming fire!

How Lovely!

How lovely lies the snow tonight
Upon a country lane;
In moonlight's touch of silver light
It glistens once again
To bring a sparkle to this time,
And diamonds to the day;
How lovely is this wondrous clime;
In whiteness, pray, do stay!

How lovely is the glitter of
The snow beneath the sun;
A wintry beauty that I love,
When children have such fun
To race down hills in snowy spills,
Their laughter laced with glee;
How lovely all these childish thrills
That seem to call to me.

But I am old and near my fire
Rethinking childhood ways;
To dreams of yesteryears aspire—
Those blissful bygone days.

. . . And Scatter Stars

Each day shall end in golden plunge
As all the days before
In cycles viewed by countless eyes,
Their legends staff the lore

Of time ago when suns burned gold;
When moons shone silver-hued;
When stars once sprinkled diamond dust;
When probing stares pursued

A comet's tail in maddened dash
Across an empty space
To disappear – where must it go?
And did it die in grace?

God, grant me one more golden day,
One blaze of silver night;
And scatter stars upon my path—
To guide me to Your Light.

A Reminder

I love the rain, its liquid grace;
In silver drops it bathes my face
And brings a lushness to a place.

When it retreats, I somehow know
That I shall rue its ebb and flow;
Horizons fade in misty glow—

In seasons when rain does not come,
I miss its throb; I miss its thrum;
My spirits sink; my heart is numb.

And comes the day when I shall die,
I'll take one peek at western sky;
And pray for rain with my last sigh—

Though I should sleep a thousand years,
I'll ask my friends to dry their tears;
And when a western storm appears—
They'll think of me.

Moon Whispers

The clouds grow soft like cotton puffs
As white as white can be;
The blue, too azure in its depth,
As far as eyes can see.

The sun, an orb of pulsing gold,
Its rays fill splendored skies;
The moon of silver face looks on
White smile of faint surprise.

And man on Earth views all these things:
The white, the blue, the gold;
And whispers to the silver moon—
His words are never told.

A Poet's Praise

Once came a winter's sparkling snow;
Once came a springtime's green;
But golden autumn I love so
To follow summer's scene;
When on the dappled hills nearby
In rays of softened touch,
A far-off sun's emblazoned sky
Paints canvas that is such

Reflection of a moment when
The brown and red and gold
Brings lyrics to a poet's pen:
Septembers long extolled
By bards who wrote a phrase of praise
Upon a season's glow;
And captured phase of autumn days
In flawless, metered flow.

Again a winter's world of snow;
Again a springtime's sheen;
Again an autumn . . . soft, aglow,
Replacing summer's green.

My True Delights

Where goes the autumn comes the snow
    In blanket fleecy white?
Where go the fiery colors, and
    Why have they taken flight?

    Where go the dusty trails I knew
        Strewn with the golden leaves?
    And suns emblazoned gone away?
        For these my old heart grieves.

Where goes the harvest moon that shone
    Against the cooler nights?
And pumpkins stacked at edge of fields?
    These were my true delights.

Where go the dear friends I had loved?
    For them my sad heart grieves;
Must they depart as if they're strewn
    On trails as autumn leaves?

Would that an autumn come again!
    Would that this world of white
Erupt in red and gold and brown!
    Indeed, a precious sight!

A Dream I've Had

I'll take a walk on snowy eve,
My thoughts profoundly deep;
Firm resolution I have made—
A promise I shall keep.

I'll count the crunches as I walk,
Attune myself to God;
Forget the biting wind, the cold,
On path that must be trod.

The snow grows deep, the woods asleep,
My thoughts shape patterns to
A dream I've had too many years:
This path I now pursue.

Reflection lulls the world asleep,
I take one step; and I've
Begun the dream I dreamt ago—
It now has come alive.

My Kingdom, Small It Be

Beneath the mists of foggy eve
There lies a garden I
Have tended with a loving touch
Beneath a once-blue sky.

Within these mists the flowers drink
Cool moisture from the dew;
And when the sun smiles from the east,
They reach for sky-kissed blue.

And with green thumb of knowing touch
I tend each flower there;
Survey my kingdom, small it be,
Renewed by misty air.

In westward glow the sun retreats,
Accedes to misty night;
My garden floats in twilight's mist;
Indeed a lovely sight.

A Place I've Never Been

The hills rise up – a bluing haze
With mist from clouds that touch upon
A snow-capped crest that reaches to
A place I've never been before;

Its face looks back in shocking glow,
Resplendent in the sun's long beams,
And settles for a moonlit sleep,
Awakens to a softened day;

And once anew the upward climb
Of fire and ice of elements;
A softness changed to hardened steel—
This crest I've never reached before;

Nor shall I ever scale these heights;
Nor hope to rest in bluing skies;
It is a place beyond my grasp—
This land I view from far below.

My Little Sparrows

Oh look! They're here again today;
Most come to eat, but others play;
But of a sudden, up, away!
My little sparrows . . .

What brings them back I cannot know;
They come in rain; they come in snow;
And with timed flutter, off they go! –
My little sparrows . . .

It does not matter spring or fall,
Or when the summer makes its call;
Or when the winter chills us all—
My little sparrows . . .

His creatures small, His creatures great,
Each one a part of kindred fate;
I rise each morning to await—
My little sparrows . . .

I do believe that one may be
A special angel He sends me;
Though filled with doubts, I think I see—
My special angel . . .

And So I Go

I wish to go where fancy roves
Upon a wistful day;
Where violet looms the twilight
As sunbeams make their play.
Where butterflies on floating wings
Glide flagrant in display;
Where shadows fade from azure skies
As they are chased away.

I wish to find an Eden's peace
Before the apple fell;
An idyll shall I sing with zest—
I know the words full well.
I wish a morning's light to fuse
With ocean's rise and swell;
And in the evening would that I
Hear call of vespers' bell.

And so I go where fancy thrives,
To land both vague and sweet;
My musings stitched in tapestries—
And thus my dream complete.

A Golden Thief

How green all things now that the rain
    Has brought its cool relief;
    When but a day or two ago
    The sun, as golden thief,

Had shone relentlessly and had
    Displayed its torrid face,
To steal the core and heart of that
    Which brings true nature's grace.

But now the soft and lustrous green
    Resides where once its brown
    Had but a day or two ago
Begged that the rain come down.

How pleased my soul now that the rain
    Has chased the golden thief;
    When but a day or two ago
    I begged for sweet relief.

In Fallen Snow

At whitened morning I shall go
To take a walk in fallen snow;
And treasure every moment which
He's given me; I feel so rich.

I'll see faint smoke as it ascends
And note the whiteness as it blends
Into the groves of powdered trees;
Espy a rabbit as it flees.

The early sun in golden glow
Enhances diamonds in the snow
To cast enchanting quietude;
Far from the throngs in solitude!

And as the day to evening sends
The colored hues as twilight ends,
I wait for sunrise; I shall go
At heightened daybreak in the snow.

A Special Time

When flowers bloom in early spring—
When autumn leaves must fall—
When summer roses reach new heights,
I dream of winter's call.
Its icy bursts of whistling winds—
Its white of driven snow—
And I at home by roaring fire;
I have no place to go.

For I'm content just where I am;
No place I'd rather be.
It is the season I await:
A special time for me.
But come the blooms of early spring—
And yes, the summer rose—
And autumn's leaves of fabled gold;
Precursors, I suppose.

But for the biting nip I yearn—
Indeed, the wintry blast
That brings me to a world unto
My dreams of winters past.

Essence Of A Season

Spring is here; it comes at last.
We soon forget cold winter's blast.
Now buds and shoots attired in green
    Are all about, you see.

Spring is here; the sun warms up.
    There is one—a buttercup!
And colts and lambs in frolic play,
    Cause kids to shout with glee.

Spring is here; it proves to man
    That of necessity a plan
Empowers all with gift of life
    Within, without . . . to be!

And So To Sleep

A silence in a glade
Surrounds two grazing deer;
Suspicious snorts, two twitching tails
Reflect their anxious fear.

What fleeting thoughts they must dispose,
Disguised in tangled brush;
They speed to deeper grove
With caution in their rush.

In darkest copse the buck stands guard
On edge with each new sound;
A nervous, regal sentry to
The peaceful haven found.

Nor beast, nor man can find their spot,
Intrude upon their keep;
And in a fearless solitude
Two creatures go to sleep.

At Home Am I

It's cold and wet and dreary, and
I'm near my warming fire;
My kettle's on and whistling low—
Of this I'll never tire.

I'm safe inside as foul winds rage;
The trees sway to and fro;
At home am I; and home I'll stay—
I have nowhere to go.

A Search For Peace

One day I'll have serenity;
I know I'll find it on
A greening hill in dappled shade,
Or where a sun has shone

To give its warmth to all near to
In beaming, pulsing rays;
To bring about a feeling that
Comes with the happy days.

For on a greening hill I'll find
This secret, dappled place;
And I shall have serenity—
The blessing of His Grace.

Beyond My Door

I love the shadows of the night
When all things secret are
Withdrawn and hidden from my sight;
Beyond my door ajar
There lurk the bogeymen I dread,
Those specters of the night
Who rove about though surely dead—
But leave at morning's light.

The World Grows Softer

As I arise to each new day
I view the sunrise, rarest gem.
A splendored scattering of light
Of golds and scarlets sent by Him.
And when the crests of highest noon
Paint azure's touch against the white
Of clouds that float on endlessly,
I see Him in this startling light.

As if by plan a sunset comes
Emblazoned on the shattered hues
Of colors only He could blend
From golds and scarlets and from blues.
And then His touch at twilight's mist:
The world grows softer as the day
Accepts the overtures of night
When golds and scarlets slip away.

Such Beauty To Behold

The slightest hint of autumn now
As summer slips away,
A cooling breeze refreshingly
Precedes a golden day.

A morning wrapped in fuzzy mist
As sunbeams fill the sky;
And of a sudden in the east
The streaking colors fly.

Dry leaves are scattered by the wind—
Some brown, and red, some gold.
The Master's art in shades I love,
Such beauty to behold.

In golden realm for scarcest time
I'll while the hours away;
While watching leaves float on the wind,
I'll bid that autumn stay.

Small Wonder

One little ray of sunshine can
Bring happiness unto
A lonely soul, a hurting heart,
Just as a sky of blue
May bid the birds to soar on high
With happiness on wing;
In bliss of full abandonment—
Small wonder they must sing!

Where Memories Grow

There is a place, a country lane,
A lovely path I know
Where in the springtime's radiance
Reflections seem to grow;

To look upon the path as though
I walked it yesterday,
Or raced with boundless, childish glee
To find my fields of play;

Today the lane, this country path,
Though but a memory
Lives for a moment radiant
For my old eyes to see;

And I reune in dreamy thought
To view this lovely sight;
Though thrust of springtime's radiance
Somehow has taken flight.

Rain Music

I'm happy only when the rain
Is whispering its song,
The drumming, strumming as it falls;
Oh would it last so long
That I could fall asleep, then rise
To hear it yet again;
No bromide here on this grand earth
Like sound of falling rain.

Windows Ablaze In Welcome

Too faint the light of partial moon,
   For shadows flit and play;
The chimney's smoke grows hesitant
   And blends to twilight's gray;

But windows ablaze in welcome;
   The nighttime drawing near;
And homeward bound am I, mere lad,
   To those I hold so dear;

Flickering lamps bid me enter
   From darkness of the night;
And the ember's glow of fireside—
   Indeed a warming sight!

And I am home! At home at last
   To this a place where I'll
Be loved and given sustenance
   For but a little while;

And then be off by circumstance
   Pursuing life's career;
But windows ablaze in welcome
   Shall always draw me here.

Not To Ends Of Earth

I shall not go to ends of earth
To find my solitude;
For I've discovered it at home,
A realm of quietude;
A place I cloak myself as if
Invisible I be;
I'm safe in my environs, and
It suits me perfectly;
No need to travel far and wide—
I have it all right here:
My quietude, my cozy nest—
All things that I hold dear.

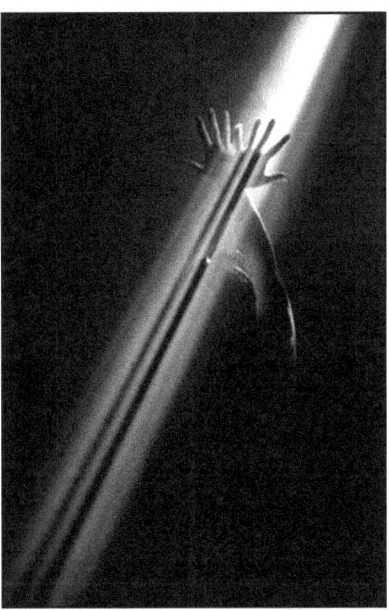

Point Of Observation

The dewy morning drips to rainy night—
And footprints in the grass belie the trail
Of one year behind another—old light
Years must traverse the cosmos and then fail

To halt a lingering sun—or a moon
Longing to leave its static orbit—fresh
To another moment, minutes too soon—
Gazing toward future dawns in mix and mesh

Of a nothingness—abandoned by men
Who open sleepy eyes and view the stars
Streaking to a swarming, clustering pen—
To pathways of battles lost and unfought wars.

I watch my time race by at princely gait,
Though I neither care nor protest my fate.

The Candle Mine

I watch the candle flicker;
Its flame lights up the room
And I, ensnared by deepest thought,
Dismiss the evening's gloom;

A beauty to the sparkling glint
As gold assails the dark,
And I, benumbed by witless thought,
Ignore the hissing spark.

The fire is gone; no flicker now;
The room evokes the shades
Of darkness as soft twilight comes—
A sense of night pervades,

And I, remiss by idle thought,
Consider my odd shrine;
With fragile hand I strike a match
To prove the candle mine.

Songs Of The Wind

Somewhere a wind chime resonates,
Its notes upon the wind;
And random meters pulse in time
And to my world they lend
The peaceful songs of solitude
Which soften as they play
The gentle scores of zephyrs that
Have come from far away
To strum the hollow pipes with puffs—
Which make the music flow—
These vagabond musicians that
I hear but do not know.

Within A Moment

Within a moment where I stood
I saw an image deeply etched
Beyond the cusp of setting sun—
And easel wide, so broad it stretched
To points too far that I viewed not
Warm colors that enveloped me;
I sensed the teeming mysteries
At edge of roaring, crashing sea.

Within this moment thus encased
In prism of unsettled state
Came then soft sirens with their calls:
My tete-a-tete with my own fate.
How then this moment where I stand
For better or for worse
To see beyond all future suns
The awesome depth of universe.

The Way Home

A road ahead invites me to
Select a left or right,
And trudge along without a thought
For it is nearing night.

The sun must set in its own realm
In orb of melting gold,
And I must ponder here and now
What actions may unfold.

In witless steps I plow ahead;
I know my home is near.
Beyond that grove a wisp of smoke—
A place that I hold dear.

Yes, I am home! The road I took—
The way too narrow—straight—
Could only bring me to this place—
To this—my garden gate.

Where Stars Have Fallen

I know that stars have fallen there,
For in illumined flight
A cascade brief of shattered hearts
Has sprinkled edge of night
In this far realm of universe
Where souls of stars retire,
A journey from an older space
Began in streaking fire

Which sent them to a hellish plunge
In gaudy majesty,
Where veils of darkness welcomed them
To worlds we'll never see.
I think one day that they shall rise
And in illumined flight
Their hearts and souls shall sprinkle dust
To light a new day's night.

Of A Sudden

Of a sudden a darkness comes
Roiled to the points of black
And whipped by winds of fury's hordes,
It cannot hold them back;

But looses them upon the land
In broad and sweeping thrusts
To rouse the atoms long at rest
In newborn storm-tossed dusts.

Of a sudden the tempest gone;
A calm is settled, quiet
On tattered face which heals itself
In new-found shades of light.

To Heaven's Edge

Within the boughs of ancient trees
The wind of time grows soft
Upon the faceless creatures there
Whose wings once soared aloft

In grandest pose on thermal rush
Which met the rigid air,
And plunged to depths from ether's zest,
Then to the trees repaired.

But often some in happenstance
Chose never to return,
And pushed themselves to Heaven's edge
And in its brightness burn.

The Final Payment

Oh, he was sanctimonious!
Holier-than-thou was he.
His flawless life harmonious—
Whatever would be would be.

He looked down his nose at others,
Sneering as they passed him by;
And, if he had had his druthers,
Would have squashed them like a fly.

In gaited stroll he palmed his cane,
Quite ready to strike a blow.
Tilted head held high, ever vain,
Wherever he chose to go.

Then one fine day his heart died out.
He fell hard upon the ground.
In weakened state he tried to shout;
He could not muster a sound.

The moral to this story is:
"At last! At last! He got his!"

When March Winds Blow

Now gust the winds of March once more;
Bright kites are soaring high.
Tails of silk whipping in the breeze
Upon the windswept sky.

Colors competing as they dash,
Zigzagging to and fro
Against the azure sky of March
They drift in rhythmic flow.

Pure freedom they all have in flight
To rise to higher place,
Then dip to earth at end of day
With attitude of grace.

The Little Ones

How precious are the little ones:
A spotted fawn in sun-kissed glade,
Its mother near at edge of wood.
The little one sleeps, unafraid.

A lanky colt now gamboling
Upon the pasture's hillside green,
Once spindly legs full-fleshed and strong,
It is a portrait to be seen.

Tiny kittens in furry pose
Cavorting in their feline play,
The world about so strange to them
Brings bold adventures each new day.

Like them I'm but a child astray
Under God's care each dawning day.

One Last Request

If I should die come a day in autumn,
Do cover me up with bright leaves of gold.
And bury me deep on a sun-splashed hill
Where I'll bide my time till the winter's cold.

If I should die come a day in winter,
Cover me up with a blanket of snow.
And bury me deep on a white-clad hill
Where I'll bide my time till the springtime show.

If I should die come a day in springtime,
Pale daffodils do scatter all around.
And bury me near to the garden's gate
Where I shall wait for His trumpet's first sound.

But should I die come a day in summer,
Please bury me beneath a shady tree.
And promise: you must come to my service.
And please, please turn on the church's A/C.

But if you cannot do any of this,
I'll never know otherwise; that's for sure.
For I'll be on my way to Glory land
Where the environs are cool, clean and pure.

To His Seasons All

Spring hears my morning worship,
Summer my noonday prayer;
Autumn my evening reflections,
Then winter . . . He's still there.

More than a man of all seasons,
He's with me each livelong day.
I go to Him with all my needs;
It's so simple! I just pray.

Perforce then each spring comes and goes;
Torrid summers no surprise,
And autumns stretch in dusty suns;
Winters exit with long sighs.

But He is here omnipresent,
Attuned to the seasons all,
Bidding them to come and go,
Each one obeying His Call.

Oh, could I be as the seasons,
Attuned to Him all in all,
Listening with both heart and soul,
Obeying His Beck and Call.

Unto A Place

Unto a sunset's wondrous glow,
Unto rare places that I know,
I wish to go there for a spell
And in due time trust all is well.
Unto the moonlight's silver face,
Unto one night of placid grace,
I wish to travel, therein rest
Within a dream that I've known best.

Unto a morning's brilliant skies,
Unto new day with vast surprise,
I wish to wake from dream-filled sleep
And marvel that I'm in His keep.
And then unto horizons which
Delight my senses and enrich
The very heart and soul of me—
I'll find the place I wish to be.

The Gift Of An Aria

I hear their songs of happiness
Upon my windowsill,
Their notes atwitter at the dawn—
I listen to them 'til
I'm up about with daily chores
And to my daily grind;
Not knowing that these little ones
Have brought me peace of mind.

God's gift to me—these tiny birds—
He gives them notes to trill,
Then bids them sing their arias
Upon my windowsill.
And of a sudden they are gone,
These precious gems take flight—
I hope to hear their twittering
Again at morning's light.

Outside My Window

To harbor all that fly unto
Its reaching limbs which touch the blue
Of skies that dazzle in the light
From suns that dim when comes the night.

Within the safety of my tree
Live both the jay and chickadee;
While red birds nest with hatching young,
The sparrow cheeps a springtime song.

But soon the autumn: leaves turn brown
And gold and red and all fall down;
The jay's blue flutters disappear;
Comes now the winter, so I fear.

When Rain Comes

When rain comes down, I am at peace,
Calmed by the fluid flow;
I try in vain to wrestle with
The showers' wake and go

About my tasks in hurried dash
From spot to covered spot;
And chide the weatherman a bit:
"It's not quite dry and hot!"

But when those days in humid siege
Assault my sweaty brow,
I think of days when rain came down—
And peace returns somehow.

What Shall I Do?

What shall I do come autumn when
The leaves begin to fall—
To lie in wait on drowsy trails
Before the wintry call

Of whistling winds with robust throats
That roar to auburn hills
Streaked by the brush of carmine's rouge
To wait the icy chills?

What shall I do? What shall I do
When trees grow bare, bereft?
I'll think of them as they once were
Before the summer left

When in a green of vibrant gloss,
They swayed to graceful breeze,
But now in grip of winter's vise,
They lose their final leaves.

And I grow sad; and I grow old—
Whatever shall I do?
I'll bide my time, and spring shall come
To bring me skies of blue.

Wishing For Winter

The grass grows green; the sun beams hot;
The sky turns blue, and I
Wish for the winter's chilling touch—
For leaden, graying sky

With snowflakes floating whitely down
To cover autumn hue;
To make my place a wonderland—
A realm long-overdue.

My kingdom's splotched in silvered sun:
The sky turns gray, and Lo!
The sleighs race by with crunching sounds;
For now! It's here! The snow!

Temporary Guests

Where are the little ones I knew
Before the wintry days
That perched upon my windowsill
In springtime's warming rays?

Where are the little ones I watched—
The sparrow and the wren—
That brought such joy to my life
But of a sudden then

Departed on their daily rounds
To come another day
And perch upon my windowsill?
But much to my dismay

Be gone again and not return;
I wonder where they go—
Perhaps they fly to Heaven's gate—
I'm sure that God must know.

Transitions

When clarions of Spring ring out,
I sense their lovely chimes;
And in my world the beauty wakes—
It is the best of times!
But Summer follows in its rush
To speed the green along;
To paint most things in verdancy—
It is but August's song!

And oh, the Autumn—fallen leaves—
In burnished lemon-brown;
And pathways swathed in red and gold—
It is but Libra's crown!
Then blows the Winter's chilling wind
In huffing, biting blast;
My world now glitters icy-white—
December's here at last!

When Summer Goes

From shades of amber's timeless glow,
From lemon-colored flight,
From crimson touch against soft suns
Its leaves displayed by light;

In spectacle of autumn's show
They settle on the floor
Of forests deep and darkly hushed—
Now closed to summer's door;

To open up a world I'd not
Believed could ever be,
When beauty flaunts its face as that
Which falls from wind-blown tree;

But oh it is a sight indeed—
These leaves when summer goes;
When autumn's grace provides me with
Its splendored words of prose.

Once Each Day

In forests deep the shadows creep
Unto a dappled glade;
And then the sun in western run
Leaves twilight's softened shade.
A measure here of treasure dear,
It happens day to day;
And then the sun in eastward run
Brings dawning's golden ray.

Of All His Gifts

I'm happiest when skies are blue,
When clouds of cotton white
Explode upon the scene and float
In random, airy flight.

When seas below in greening hue
Stretch forth so endlessly
And touch upon a foreign strand;
Indeed, a sight to see.

When hills and valleys thrust unto
The mountains' snowy realms,
The view becomes bedazzled by
A gem that overwhelms.

Of all these things—these precious gifts—
He gives without demand,
I'm happiest when I can feel
His Presence near to hand.

When Sunset Comes

It seems to set the sky on fire;
And in a patterned dive
It gently bows from daytime stint
To chafe the night alive.

The screaming shards of color that
Succumb to violet hues
Erase the puffy clouds of white,
Deny the startling blues.

And on this scene a golden orb
Dips slowly at the rim:
At twilight in its fading glow—
It's then I think on Him.

The Splendor Of His Might

The glimmer of an evening's birth
On twilight's mist of purple haze
Soon lost within a prism's heart
To pulse within the endless days.
Ensuring countless hours to come:
Mornings and evenings to be free
For brighter daybreaks bursting forth—
Then dimming orbs perchance shall flee.

Within the promise of God's plan
A bounty's gift of precious days
Of prism in its gracious pose
On which the sunlight softly plays.
And should tomorrow be the last,
Should timed regrets be sent away—
I'll praise Him for His splendor's might
And ask Him for just one more day.

A Symphony: Rain Music

When the rain comes, when the rain drums,
When the air grows softened by
The floating silk of a dampened breeze,
When the land and sea and sky
Are blended to a metered flow
Of dust and spray and light—

Then I am home where my roof thrums
With rain sounds through the night.

Upon The Pines

Upon the pines the snow lies white,
And from a distance silver light
Luminesces; and in its glow
Creates faux diamonds in the snow.

A sunrise beams as broad array
In thrusting streaks of grand new day;
A prism's glint in wayward breeze,
Rare jewels sparkle in the trees.

Too soon! Too soon the setting sun,
So grandiose—a golden run;
Upon the pines its gleam, its glow—
How lovely this, my world of snow.

Upon this land the touch of night—
Upon the pines my day takes flight.

Time Passage

I fear the wind is cold today
As skies grow deeply blue and clear.
Another year! December gone!
How fast the hours disappear.

I know the sun reflects the soul
Of landscapes' froth of fallen snow.
See now the glow? When did it start?
How fast the seasons come and go!

To My World Of White

The snow is falling feather-light,
And in scarce moment all turns white.
The reds grow vivid, greens more green,
A time awaited: winter's scene.

And soon a drift of patterned snow,
A peaceful ebb, a movement's flow,
The flakes have ceased; the sky bright blue
Turns world of white to azure hue.

And sunset as a glitter's spark,
Emblazoned rays and then the dark.
A silver moon (where does it go?)
As sprinkling stars light up the snow.

And in my cozy cottage I'm
Safe and warm 'gainst this wintry clime;
For I shall wake to world of white.
Will snow be falling feather-light?

Within

Within my heart a tuneful lilt!
Whatever can go wrong?
And come each day it's all full tilt;
I sing that day's new song.

Within my soul a hopeful praise
Of brighter sun and sky;
And come the dawns of newer days?
None happier than I!

Until The Spring

If I should leave you come the spring
Be not afraid for me
For I shall tarry but a while
Beneath that grand old tree
Whose boughs must shelter me as time
Fades to a destiny
And I shall lie in sweet repose
Beneath that grand old tree

If I should leave on summer's day
Grant me that peaceful place
Where I shall bide till God calls me
To bask in His Fair Grace
Which shall, as promised, see me through
To countless autumns of
The years to come before I shall
Be in His Endless Love

But if I part on wintry day
Please! Please no show of grief—
For I shall wait for briefest time
Till comes His Springtime Leaf.

Pipe Dreams

One day I'll take my leave and go
Unto a cloud-kissed peak
Where snows may come at any time
And where the angels tweak

The stars of splendor hung aloft
Like tinseled Christmas lights;
Where deepened skies of azure hue
Absorb the moonlit nights.

Where days are endless, if you wish;
Where suns turn off and on;
Where satin moons at one's request
Change to emblazoned dawn.

In peace I'll rest with fretless ease
In this—a place I dreamed—
And find my world as I viewed it
Was not what it had seemed.

Of Gracious Days

September dares to pose itself
In summer's path to all
The leaves that turn in golden mists,
As autumn comes to call;

October, shot with streaking flames
Of red and gold and brown,
And lemon, too, in graceful flight—
The leaves come wafting down;

November, fringed with nipping cool,
For fall is everywhere;
A quietude of gracious days—
Thanksgiving's in the air;

Then of a sudden winter blows;
The snows are piling high;
I think of autumn's calming hush—
A season passes by . . .

Of A Woodland Scene

So gray the sky and dismal, and
The rain is falling near;
All creatures seeking shelter now;
How can they disappear?

What primal urge tells them to flee?
And where must they all go?
And look! The rain is changing to
A lace-like, falling snow.

Now on the woodland glazed in white
Too hushed, too calm, serene;
Still gray the sky, but beautiful
This placid, wintry scene.

God is the Giver of all gifts:
His sky of leaden gray—
His creatures seeking shelter and
A special winter day.

One Wonders Where They Go

It's wintertime! The country lanes
With wind-blown layered snow
In drifts so high, old paths unclear;
One wonders where they go.

A cedar dressed in touch of white;
A lovely Christmas tree?
And holly bush with berries red—
What else is there to see?

The lofty pines like sentinels
Watch o'er the pensive deer;
On eastern winds the barks of hounds—
Could they be coming near?

A nervous bunny tests the air
From snowbank on a hill;
And red birds dart in perky flights
Across untrodden field.

A cottage in the distance with
Its chimney's plume of gray;
And warming lights from windows that
Defy the chilling day.

Of Autumn's Flair

Each autumn lures me to a place
In which I pause, then walk
In dusty mists to edge of wood;
I have no cause to talk.
A muted music in the air
Threads in an evening breeze;
And of a sudden dappled light
Plays off once unseen trees.

The mists perforce seek dusty flight
In motes upon the air;
It is September's golden life—
A gift of autumn's flair.
But then a twilight's purpled glow
Replaces dappled light;
It's at this moment that the sun
Fades to an autumn night.

And I am wont to stand and watch
A drama disappear;
Enraptured and allured to this:
A season I revere.

This, The Season

A wispy smoke, a golden haze,
A burnished sun come autumn days;
A burst of flame on distant hills
As season's winds bring dusty chills.
Bright pumpkins stacked by shocks of corn
In dewy pose at early morn;
And night birds flee in fluttered flight
To seek their shelter ere the night.

A village bell tolls end of day;
A farmer wends his weary way
Toward hearth and home and sweet repose
As western skies strike daily close.
Golden autumn: no sweeter time
Than poignant days of fairest clime;
September's gift, October's glow—
Comes this the season I love so.

Children: Their Special Time

There rings a song of happiness
   Upon this April day,
As children in the blush of spring
   Grow busy in their play;
While flowers bloom upon the lea
   Or drowse in warming sun,
It is a special time of year
   When children have great fun.

Long past the windy blows of March
   When kites were meant to fly;
Long past the wintry throes of ice
   When snow was drifting high;
I'll hear the songs of happiness
   Upon an April day;
No youngster I, though child I am
   Recalling fields of play.

Night Music

How patiently the night sounds wait
For western skies to close
Upon a day in slow retreat;
Too ploddingly it goes.
But patience wins the hour at last
As one by one the notes
In music to nocturnal ears
Upon the night air floats.

In full crescendo rises to
A dome of twinkling light;
Cacophonies aspire and vie
To echo through the night.
What sounds be these upon the air?
What plaintive night birds sing?
Cicadas vex their sawing rhymes;
Raw rhapsody they bring.

In measured climb but for a spell
A symphony to night;
But at the dawn of eastern sun—
Musicians out of sight.

To Heaven They Aspire

In time all roses seem to climb
And reach toward awkward skies;
And in a silken moment grant
A treasure of surprise
That such a thing so beauteous
And queenly in attire,
Might in its full regalia
To Heaven so aspire.

A fragrant mist upon the edge
Of season's balmy air,
It wafts away unto the night
And finds a moonbeam's care;
Then morning breaks—the sun erupts
To share its glow of gold;
And roses open up their hearts—
A glory to behold.

The Hush Looms Soft

The hush looms soft and white and cold
From meadow to the wood;
The air uplifts with bracing nip;
Indeed, I think I should
Prepare to forge a journey and
Bestir myself today;
Horizons far in bluing mists
Allure and point my way.

But I am calmed by wintry hush
As worlds of sheer delight
From meadow to the nearby wood
Seem somehow to invite
A trip beyond the floating mists;
Beyond the white and cold;
Beyond the crystal realms of ice,
But I am less than bold.

And so I'll stay beside my hearth,
A coward, I suppose;
The hush looms soft and white and cold
And now the north wind blows.

Who We Are

I'll think of dew-kissed bluebells when
    The morning sun should rise;
And picture tender violets that
    Bring pleasure to my eyes.

I'll wait for thermal winds to sweep
    From dusty western plains;
And search for thunder clouds that hint
    Of drenching, cleansing rains.

I'll love the daffodils that grow
    Where once a brave heart stood;
I'll stop; admire a rose and then
    Find respite in a wood.

It is of nature who we are,
    And who we strive to be;
I'll dwell upon these lovely thoughts
    To find the inner me.

That All Be Well

At rainbow's end—Oh! Where is it?
Why must these clouds of gray
In pulsing rhythms spawn the rains,
Bright sun in fact betray?

It soon must show; I know it will—
That arc of iris hue
Which in an instant far away
Upon horizons blue

Displays God's Wish that all be well;
His Rainbow makes it so—
In colors fused, how pleasant they
In metered ebb and flow

Caress one's spirit and align
One's heart as if on cue
At rainbow's end—Oh! There it is!
God's Promised Iris Hue.

Sunrise: Within The Magic Dust

It's pink in eastern skies, but yet
Where is expected gold?
Beneath horizons, endlessly
It reaches I am told . . .

Rare marvels that await the eye
Within the magic dust
Now bide their time and at command
Explode; I'm sure they must . . .

For in the glory that shall be
The pink shall cede its hold;
And in a raptured moment then,
God's skies shall burst in gold.

Think Of The Autumns

Think of the morning mists of fall
Upon the golden leaves
When sunrise chases nighttime shade
To glow upon the sheaves;
Proud sentinels in dusty fields
By farmers' hands aligned;
Think of the beauty spread about,
September's redefined.

Think of a burnished sky at dusk
Unto a twilight's span
When sunset bids the daylight fade
As part of nature's plan.
Think of dim autumns of ago;
They came another day;
As memories, though here again,
Have opted not to stay.

When Once The Rain

How green the land when once the rain
    Had fallen for a spell;
    Enchanted flowers came alive
    And graced a wishing well.

A velvet softness stirred the air
    With fragrance near divine;
    And what was dry a time ago
    Grew verdant and was mine.

Once A Gentle Breeze

The whisper of a breeze is heard
As twilight's purple haze
Eclipses gold of setting sun,
Erasing final rays;

Then sudden music from the trees
On zephyr's sweetened notes
Caresses leaves with gusty rush,
And on the warm air floats.

Within a trice a symphony
Where once a gentle breeze
As whispered music had begun—
Mere movement in the trees.

In roaring swells, crescendo now,
This orchestra of night;
Where once a subtle whisper heard—
The sun falls out of sight.

Where Bluebells Grace The Spring

Where welcomed rains are pattering
Upon a windowpane;
Where striking bluebells grace the spring
But wake to bloom again

When leaves of gold blow scattering
Upon the autumn ground;
Where old and muted church bells ring,
So velvety their sound

That I shall ache to see again
The faces of ago;
My tears of pleasure mixed with pain:
These truths I dare to know.

It's fact that I shall dream again
Should bluebells come to call;
But now I'll peer through misted pane
And watch the raindrops fall.

Once Stood A Church

Where once a stained-glass window rose
To touch a cobalt sky;
Where splintered scarlets from a sun
Brought colors to defy
The master strokes of artists who
Sought perfection's blended hue;
Who strove to match a beauty that
Outshone their own purview.

Where once the sunlight beamed to fall
Upon a polished floor;
Where dappled flecks of gold had danced
Upon the vestry's door
Where once an organ scaled to heights
In notes of mellow flow;
Where songs of praise to Heaven soared
From harmonies below.

Now but a shell, it rises to
A graying, distant sky;
And in its void, its emptiness,
One asks the question: "Why?"

Of Blue On Blue

I think the sky must reach unto
An endless end of blue on blue;
Or could it end? I don't think so;
It seems to me to go and grow
To depth, to breadth of universe,
Which always to new fronts disperse;
Eternal be odd building blocks
Unhampered by poor earthly clocks.

What a pittance: three score and ten,
The time accorded to some men;
I think these years must reach unto
The blue on blue which all pursue.

On Summer Day

How lovely glows a springtime day
When flowers bloom in vast array;
When breezes stir the grand oak trees,
When birds trill out in harmonies;

When grasses gleam on hill and dale;
When skies turn blue and all seems well;
When storm clouds melt with rainbow's arc;
When twilights fade to rush of dark.

How strong I grow on spring-like day
In foolish pleasure and in play;
For in its thrust and in its bloom
My heart transcends the deepest gloom.

And on a breeze my soul, bestirred,
Flows like rare silk on each new word;
Horizons pulse then float away;
How lovely goes my summer day!

The Face Of Twilight

When twilight dons its shadowed veil,
The skies turn soft in hued pastels;
A retrospect in pensive trace
Benumbs the aura of a place
Which on one bright and golden day
In velvet touch had held full sway;
But wilted as the sun set low
In sacrifice to satin glow.

I lived this day in time well-spent;
How peaceful I in hours' content
To watch the shadows creep unto
The woodland's edge; and then the dew
In crystal glaze succumbed to night;
And in skies deep the silver light
Of moon once hidden could release
The fleeting face of twilight's peace.

Springtime Art

A lilt is in the air and I
Must sing the songs that tell
The world I know that April's here
To stay for just a spell;

A mellow time when green takes hold
And flowers touch the dew;
When showers come on April's terms
And rainbows fill my view;

But then along comes Merry May;
Her presence paints the land
In colors rife in prism's glint,
Each shown at her command;

And now I know why April comes
And brings its showers to
Renew the hope for springtime art
Against May's skies of blue.

Each month a part and parcel of
This spring that comes my way;
A lilt is in the air, and I
Shall savor each new day.

The Wonder Of A Wintry Day

A graying fog on distant hills
Muffles the chimes of far-off spire;
While I am home safe from the chills
Before my roaring, warming fire;

Where are the lanes? They've disappeared,
Covered by snow as I had feared;
No jingling sleighs—too deep the snow—
So all stay home, no place to go;

The fogs have lifted! And the sky
Too blue, too shocking to an eye
That's seen but naught the shades of gray;
Oh! The wonder of wintry day

When I am home safe to my fire,
Removed from threat of wind-blown chills,
I hear the chimes from far-off spire
And see the skies flame distant hills.

Wanderlust

To savor every second and
Be free as butterflies;
To float in splendid elegance
In lure of azure skies;

To break the bonds of world I know;
Be free to wander, and
To walk upon a coral beach
And touch its pinkish sand;

To visit places only seen
By those who choose to roam;
To see a house in winsome glow,
And say, "I know I'm home."

To live my life to full degree;
Rise up as morning sun,
Become a part of rainbow's arc—
Now wouldn't that be fun?

But in the meantime I think that
I'll take life's passing day;
And relish moments as they come—
Is there a better way?

To Other Worlds

It is a bit of heaven that
I cherish come the spring,
When first I hear the robin's call:
No other bird dare sing;

As harbinger, as promise of
A season yet to be;
An April with warm showers that
Bring budding to each tree;

Its clarity of song is heard
With lyrics full of cheer;
And fills the corners of my world,
This grandest time of year;

And then away to parts unknown
To sing robustly there;
The robin flies to other realms—
Its springtime song to share.

Upon A Deepened Night

September's fade; October's glow;
November's mist in gray
Of skies which once in azure bursts
Had blessed a summer day;

And ceded to a primal call
Against a silver light
To bring the moon to chilling glimpse
Upon a deepened night;

But then it faded straightaway;
December came to be;
And nearing to a woodland's edge—
A bending snow-draped tree;

But in mind's eye I see the fall:
September fades and goes—
October glows; November mists—
Now come December's snows.

While Idlers Sleep

Upon the sleeping glade a mist lies thin,
Though in a space of time its veil shall wane;
And dancing colors, bold and bright and brushed,
Shall whir the air with vivid life again.
For then the hordes of those in movement dash
From vantage gained by days in other suns;
While idlers sleep these doers ply their trades,
Invest poor effort in these daily runs.
Upon the sunset's face the glow lies dulled,
For in a span the colors bleed and run;
Unto the sleeping night a voice cries out:
"How can this be what mankind leaves undone?"

With Sled In Tow

It's wintertime! The snow comes down
   On country lanes, on streets in town;
   With dazzling coats of chilling white
     It blankets everything in sight;

   And takes me back so long ago
When leaden skies brought our first snow.
   We raced to slopes of nearby hills
   And with delight we took our spills

   And sledded 'til the sun went down
   Behind the mountains far from town.
   Then in the evening's afterglow,
   We plodded home, our sleds in tow.

   I'll dream a dream of wintry eve
   When I shall take my sled and leave
My fireside warmth for childhood thrills
   On snow-clad slopes of nearby hills.

And Winter comes with its first snow—
   I'll be a child with sled in tow.

No Final

When I must die, let it be fall
When leaves of brown and gold
And brightest red rest on my head . . .
As I shall lay me down.

When I must die, allow the winds
Blow sharp and brisk and cold
Let reaching sun touch everyone . . .
And bathe my lifeless crown.

But should I die in springtime
As April turns to May
When bursting earth explodes in birth . . .
Not one word will I say.

So if I die in summer's heat
Or on a wintry date
I'll have no voice in this last choice . . .
Alas, the wiles of fate!

Softly, A Promise

A softness on the April hills
Shot through by splintered sun
Greens up in valleys stretching forth
With kiss of showers' run.

Comes May enchantress once exiled
To brush the earth with shades
Of green in forests deeply dark,
She rests in leafy glades.

With splendid eyes she daubs her paint,
Enchants the land once more
With kingdoms ruled by lords of green
Near to my cottage door.

And I, who thought all worlds long dead
To frozen days grown bleak,
View promised hints of greenery
Upon a snow-capped peak.

Sweet Bells Sing Out

The bells ring out; my spirits soar;
Their clanging fills the air;
Their dulcet tones reverberate
Beyond the village square.

It's morning now; I hear their call;
My world awakens to
Be up about its busyness,
Though robed in crystal dew.

The midday sun floats high above
While bells peal out at noon;
My frantic world takes pause to rest,
Odd hours spent too soon.

At eventide my world slows down;
The close of day draws near;
Sweet bells sing out at sun's retreat,
A song I love to hear.

That I May Say Good-bye

Where did the fading rainbow go
    Behind unsettled sky,
Beyond horizons dark and deep,
    Where did the rainbow die?

Where is the rainbow as I write,
    Its colors stretched across
The prisms of both time and space,
    Will I redeem my loss?

I bid the rainbow come once more
    That I may say good-bye
To dreams of finding pot of gold,
    A rainbow-chaser I!

Ongoing Blessings

A dawning ray of sunshine and
A little bit of rain;
A rose or two in summer, but
Dear Lord, not too much pain.

The golden leaves of autumn and
A season's dusty chill;
And comes the first of winter's snow,
Its whiteness icy thrill.

For then the year is over and
A new one 'round the bend;
And next the rush of springtime's thrust—
Such blessings does God send!

Somewhere

Somewhere a sunset fades away
Somewhere a night is born
Somewhere a blazing sun erupts
Upon a dewy morn

Somewhere the oceans pull away
Somewhere the rivers flow
Somewhere the icebergs groan and crack
In places I can't go

Somewhere an April turns to May
Somewhere October's gold
Somewhere a wintry spectacle
As ice and snow take hold

Somewhere beyond galactic fire
Somewhere beyond the dark
Somewhere near to His Heaven's Glow
One day I shall embark

These Lovely Clouds

Where do they go when they float by—
These puffy ships in azure sky?
I know no answers, nor can I
Imagine when, or where, or why
They sail from west to east; then fade
Into horizons dimmed in shade;
Perforce they go as God has bade:
These lovely clouds that He has made.

Who Else But God?

A canopy of leaves much like
A bridge of vibrant hue
That spans without restraint across
The wind-swept world of blue;
In red and orange and lemon zest
To touch the drying land;
Who else but God could ordain this:
An autumn on demand?

Too soon the canopy fades out;
The trees in barren stance
Against the chill of dusty days
As leaves are blown by chance;
To drift against a split-rail fence
Before the winter's snow;
Who else but God with His Sure Hands
Could chart this ebb and flow?

Symphony At Twilight

When twilight falls, I listen to
The sounds at hush of night:
The crickets' clatter at the edge
Of wood at first moonlight;

The plaintive call of night bird there—
Could it be mourning dove?
The piercing yelps of unseen fox—
Some of the sounds I love.

The flap and swoosh of great horned owl
That wings from tree to tree;
A barking dog, meowing cat—
These are the sounds for me.

When twilight fades to night, it seems
A symphony takes place;
God brings His music of the night—
His heartened notes of grace.

The River . . . As It Flows

Be calm and hear the music of
The river as it flows
To unknown oceans, unknown seas,
Wherever it now goes;

It is a rite of circumstance
To heed the ebb and flow;
Crescendo made by water's roar,
Wherever it may go;

A singing breeze, a whistling wind,
Streaked lightning to and fro;
Be calm and listen to these sounds—
This music I love so;

For God is Good; and God is Great;
A fact, indeed that's so!
Be calm and listen for His voice—
He is the river's Flow!

Though But A Misty Isle

Once more the rainbow's end I seek,
Though but a misty isle
Enshrouded in a splendrous glow,
A place where I may while
The hours away in retrospect;
Such manna for my soul!
An iris tinge enveloped in
A world that makes one whole.

In mist, in spray, in raindrops' fall
The spectrum's shadings blend
In opposition to the sun;
Oh must it ever end!
A vista with its threads outspun—
As jewels richly laid;
Again the rainbow's end I seek—
To know what God has made.

Truthful Colors

(In angry black of storms that rage
In snow-clad trees of white
In silver of the highest noons
In purple glow at night
In rosy dawns when breezes stir
In mist of April days
In prism's glint to deepest space
In golden sunset's rays
In yellow kiss of daffodils
In lilacs' velveteen
In roseate touch of shattered clouds
In springtime burst of green)—

How could these colors not be true?
And why, indeed, His Skies of Blue?

Sweet Autumn

And soon the sweetest time of year
When pungent wisps of smoke appear,
When skies soar high and blue and clear—
So comes the autumn . . .

When dust reflects the golden light
Of red-brown tints of leaves in flight;
When I am awed by each new sight—
So comes the autumn . . .

God's blessings rest upon the land
With harvest time at His command;
And plenitude with His sure hand—
He gives us autumn . . .

It is a season I love so
When comes the first of spitting snow;
And down a country lane I go—
He brings us autumn . . .

Reflective time for thoughtful praise
For drenching rains, for sunny days;
For greening April, luscious Mays—
Thank God for autumn . . .

Pleasant Loom The Hours

How pleasant looms the morning when
The sun is coming up,
And gentle breezes seem to rouse
The sleeping buttercup;

And of a sudden all about
A myriad of sound;
And in the distance near the wood
Pearled dew upon the ground;

My world awakes and stirs to life—
It is a special day;
How pleasant loom my hours to come
As seconds sweep away;

And I'm aware of blessing which
Come with these mornings when
I rise to greet God's splendid suns—
The happiest of men!

To Know At Heart

The pearly glint on morning dew—
The softened twilight's glow—
The shattered flame that streaks the sun—
The white of fallen snow . . .

The vibrant spring and summer days—
The autumn's burnished gold—
The brilliant clarity of ice—
The winter's bracing cold . . .

These special things He brings to me—
I know at heart that He must be.

Upon An April Day

Once ebbed a vein of springtime in
The wintry winds that blow,
That robed themselves in icy guise
Assaulting season's snow;

But in their core a crystal heart
Aspired to pulse again,
Awaited touch of unknown force—
To melt as falling rain.

Oh it was splendor never seen
Until an April day,
Tossed by the winds of March, was it,
As winter hied away.

Now spring is here—as it should be—
This promised cycle of
A time God wakes all things to life:
This season of His Love.

Within His Grandeur

Soft clouds drop low to touch the hills
As if they wish to hide
Intrusive peaks dressed white by snow
Which through the winter bide
Their time until a warming sun
Shall push the chill away
And beam the clouds to cirri-form
Above the April day

And once again the blue divides
The heavens from below
And mountains rise to majesties
That only they can know
At home am I in this domain
Within the grandeur of
These sights that only God can give
As tokens of His Love.

On A Golden Note

The day dawns cold and gray, but yet
I know the sun shall rise
To paint the world in elegance
And fill my sullen skies

With fleecy clouds embraced by light
Against a blue too deep
In perfect ceremony that
Bids hidden stars to peep

From twinkling Edens high above
To show me that my day
Now ending on a vibrant note—
Had started cold and gray.

This World Of Mine

This world of mine lies sleeping in
A wintry bed of snow
And rests in peaceful solitude
Awaiting spring, I know.

It basks in warming rays of gold
From sun at hillock's crest
And bides the savage winter chill
Until at spring's behest

A fragile touch of green is seen
Beneath the melting snow,
And in a perfect moment, God
Commands the bud to grow—

To thrust its heart in April's bliss
And fill the drowsy air—
With perfume from exotic world
In this—my season fair.

One Only Has To Listen

Now listen to the ripple of
The waters as they flow
To ends of earth behind old trees;
To distant lands they go

To breathe new life to desert place
Or nurture thirsty rose
Or kiss cold rocks, then babble on—
Forever, I suppose.

Part II:
This!
His Reasons!

Within My Heart

He lives! I know He does !
I hear His Voice today;
I hear it in the songs that ring
From children at their play.

And in the crashing waves
Of oceans' swirling foam,
I hear the rushing of His Tide
Inviting me "Come home!"

And in a mirrored light
When seeking cooling shade,
I hear the whispers of His Breeze
At edge of restful glade.

Come morning – I awake;
I hear His Voice once more.
It heralds true beginnings of
The life I have in store.

He lives! I know He does!
Or else I could not be.
He lives within the hearts of all—
Within my heart is He!

Directions

His peace I seek in morning's mist
And in an evening's glow;
And in the blaze of noonday's sun,
His calm I need to know

In patterns which direct my soul
And guide me toward His light;
Secure, at peace, I make my way
To meet the awkward night.

Rare thing, indeed, His gift of peace—
More treasured than a gem;
But ever there for anyone
Who reaches out to Him.

For He is there in morning mist
And in the evening glow—
Within the blaze of noonday sun—
Wherever we may go.

The Ascent

To reach the highest mountaintop,
To scale a frozen peak,
To reach for stars beyond the blue—
But Oh Lord! I am weak
Lord, push me upward! Up! Up! Up!
Where breath is thin and rare.
Then push me more and tell me that
You love me and I'll dare

To reach new heights with little fear,
And view majestic world.
You'll offer much but only if
I leave Your flag unfurled.
But Lord, I've told You I am weak;
I need Your Guiding Light
To splinter darkness just ahead,
To pierce the heavy night.

With You I'll scale the frozen peak;
I'll touch Your Stars one day;
I'll reach Your highest mountaintop
Where I shall stop to pray.

A World Of Serendipity

One gives no thought to asking for
The things beyond one's need;
And in the process of this act
Commits to selfish greed.

Not what one needs; but what one wants,
Divisive in its scope;
And in the rancor of this math
It tots up selfish hope.

Why not by accidental means
Discover things not bought?
With serendipity receive
A priceless gift unsought?

Friendship

Who are my friends? I think I know.
They're those who set my heart aglow
In deeds and acts that somehow show
Their willingness to share warm smile,
And walk with me my troubling mile.

They lend a hand and gladly share
Their own abode with cupboard's fare,
And lift me up and not compare
My failures to someone's success,
Nor gripe about the added stress.

Who are my friends? I know I know.
They're those who set my soul aglow
With deeds and acts that truly show
Their willingness to laugh and smile,
And hold my hand that troubled mile.

Old friends! Old friends! I'll treasure them.
As diamonds rough, or priceless gem.
I'll hold them close when they depart;
We've prized each other from the start.
(For we are one in soul and heart).

From A Seed

A seed of doubt must ever sprout
And grow into a weed;
But as it grows, its true hate shows
And spawns its own misdeed.

Remove the seed and kill the weed
To exorcise all doubt.
Without, within, among all men:
True love will winnow out.

Always Near

He's never very far away;
He's in the splendored light
When sunbeams chase the darkness that
Had harbored depth of night.

He's in the blazing light of noon;
He's in the sunset's glow
When colors of magnificence
Display His ebb and flow.

And in the course of daily life
I know I'll find Him where
The dimming sun greets twilight's shade;
Within my whispered prayer.

And in the evening's purple haze,
And in the shadowed night,
I know tomorrow He'll be there—
Eternal is His Light.

Faith: Partially Defined

A mustard seed, a grain of sand,
A mouth to feed, events unplanned;
A blazing sun, a night of cold,
No place to run as hours unfold.

A village scene, a song I know,
As apple green, a drift of snow;
A ship to sail, a note to write
That all bodes well as comes the night.

A child abed, a river's edge,
A curly head, a dusty ledge;
A hunting dog on springtime day
Into the woods it leads the way.

A lifetime's love, a wrinkled face,
The stars above, each one in place;
And I am guided as He planned
Like mustard seed, like grain of sand.

A Pause For Thanks

I pause a moment as the sun
Is rising in the east
To think of things I'm thankful for—
His Blessings not the least.

So many wonders come to mind;
The laughter of a child,
A streaking star in midnight skies,
Or wintry day turned mild.

Resounding cries of raucous jays
(Perhaps I came too near);
Or of a greening meadow there
Where daffodils appear;

A soaring kite, a billowed sail,
A cup of warming tea;
A clock chimes two in village square
Though it is really three.

A day of health and happiness,
A night of sweet repose;
A robin's song to herald spring,
The essence of a rose.

And so my day goes swiftly by;
I cannot name all things
That give due purpose to my life
And joy that each brings;

I pause a moment as the sun
Fades slowly in the west;
I count my blessings, thankful that
Each new one seems the best.

In The Fullness Of Time He Came

In the fullness of time He came
To change sinful lives evermore.
Preplanned the Glory of His Name,
And wondrous the wonders in store.

To walk upon the face of earth,
To abide among sinful men;
To come to us in lowly birth
And give up his own life, and then

Rise again to His Father's right,
Act as intercessor for all;
Glow forever as Shining Light
And hear each sinner's prayerful call.

I, in my journey here below,
Shall mark the fullness of each day;
And when I rise at dawn to go
About my dull work, I shall pray:

"How wondrous the wonders in store!
How wondrous that my Savior came!"
I'll praise His Glory evermore
In the fullness of His Great Name.

In The Broad Scheme

In the broad scheme of things I know
Christ offers His Great Love to me.
The best I can do? Accept it.
No! No strings attached: it is free.

How simple His plan for us all;
Yet too simple for some to see.
They overlook His graciousness,
His Sacrifice for you and me.

To be forgiven is one thing;
One's sins completely washed away.
The best we can do? Just ask Him
All you have to do is to pray.

In Preparation Of

Prepare me, Lord! Show me the way
That leads to eternal life.
Prepare me, Lord! Teach me to pray
And defuse my daily strife.

Urge me on, Lord! Oh, I am weak,
And I need You all the time.
Urge me on, Lord, that I may seek
The haven of Heaven's clime.

As I near promised golden hour
Give me strength to take last breath.
Sanctioned by Your wondrous power—
All I need to face my death.

Lord, with You I shall be, and then,
Embraced in Your loving arms,
Free from all strife, free from all sin,
And free from all earthly harms.

A Perfect Plan Ignored

How can some folk not realize
How simple salvation's plan?
Christ gave His Life upon the cross,
Erased every sin of man,

And died the death for all of us
So we can stand proudly free
From Satan's clutch once and for all.
Yes! Christ died for you and me!

How can one not see perfection
Of God's perfect, perfect plan?
Arrogant are we, I confess,
Each of us a sinful man.

But He will forgive one and all
If one asks Him to do so.
His Plan is all-encompassing,
But to His Cross we must go.

Both Great And Small

When I grow sad, I feel His hands,
His touch, His nudge; He understands
My heart, my needs, unspoken prayer—
I know indeed, that He must care.

If I should fall in error's way,
He always sends a brighter day;
Within the clouds His rainbow's arc—
His Guiding Light when it grows dark—

Or in a forest's dappled glade,
Or in a great oak's evening shade,
I know He tends both great and small—
For He's the Master over all.

So why is it that I grow sad
Despite the blessings I have had?
My daily moods swing to and fro—
I know He cares: His Truth is So.

My Heart Can't Wait

My heart can't wait; it longs to soar
To heights I've never reached before;
It yearns to surge with ardent zeal,
To ache when scaling highest hill;

It pines for days of long ago,
When in the tides of ebb and flow
It pulsed in agony of youth
And sought the glow of shining truth;

My heart can't wait; it longs to fly
To edges of the farthest sky;
And in that aftermath glide to
The deepest of the bluest blue;

And though its days grow numbered now,
It somehow lengthens to allow
A <u>joie</u> <u>de</u> <u>vivre</u>, not less – but more!
My heart shan't wait; it longs to soar.

Where Do I Go?

Where do I go when I'm afraid?
A secret place I know
Where I am safe in comfort's arms—
This is the place I go;

Where do I go when I'm unsure?
A special place I've found
Where I am given answers that
Lead me to solid ground;

Where do I go when I am sad?
A happy place I've known
These many years – a haven that
To no one I have shown;

No need for me to be afraid,
Nor should I be unsure;
No pangs of sadness should I bear—
God shares his Love so pure;

And I abide with confidence;
No doubts assail me there—
His shelter all-encompassing—
Indeed, His Love foursquare.

Wherein My Spirit Bides

Within Whose Heights all answers come
In perfect harmony,
Discordant not a word of choice—
Each sound a reverie.

An echo of a time ago
Of perfect love's release,
When in a light transcendent came
The Prince of Perfect Peace.

Within Whose Depths my spirit bides
In harmony and calm,
Concordant is this world of choice—
In perfect healing balm.

No Steps Retraced

To walk a mile un-walked before
Is meeting up with God
Who made it all as it is seen,
A place no one has trod;

Nor shall again as it is now,
Unlike it was before;
No steps retraced; no steps un-walked;
They must be less, not more.

But oh to find a path again—
To find a way untrod—
To walk along in silence, and
Take time to talk to God.

The Master's Touch

In ways I cannot see or know
There comes the Master's touch;
He reaches far beyond these depths;
I cannot fathom such

As in His April greening that
Erupts upon the land
He brings new life from barren scapes;
So deft the Master's hand;

To grand His cornucopia,
His plenitude replete;
And sated is my every wish
Despite the summer heat;

But when He casts cold winter's face,
I sense His closure to
His autumn with its dusty gold—
His seasons fade on cue.

He grants those things we cannot know,
Those things we cannot see;
His touch is omnipresent in
His seasons' mystery.

When My Heart Is Ready

I know He hears me when I pray
Though silent be my voice;
He numbs the pain within my heart
And bids my soul rejoice.

In comfort's glow I think on Him;
My heart talks to Him, and
I sense His presence, feel His Touch;
I know His nail-scarred Hand.

For He is never far from me:
A silent thought away;
And when my heart is ready, I'm
Prepared to pause and pray.

Reflections

It is a time of studied pause;
It is an hour when I
Reflect upon His gifts to me—
Those things I cannot buy.

It is a time for thankful thoughts;
It is a moment when
I give full praise for what I have—
Forget what might have been.

It is a time I must commend:
This special hour of prayer—
These minutes which assure me that
I'm ever in His care.

Never Mine

A passion which I have and hold
As credit to ensure
That fingers of my hand shall write
Some lines that may endure

Another day, a thousand years,
Until the suns decline;
These words evade me even now—
But they were never mine.

To Find Less-Travelled Way

Comes now a shady pathway where
I walk to find surcease
From stress of daily problems that
Disturb my inner peace.
I wander through a sun-flecked scape
Enrobed in softened light;
I chat with God; He tells me that
All things will be all right.

My heart exults in joyous beat
To know that He is near
In moments that I need Him most—
He is the One Who hears.
I listen to His words of calm,
Forget my taxing day;
And in the aura of His Peace,
I find less-travelled way.

A Child Of Boundless Grace

Mary! Mary! Do hold Him tight
And swaddle Him against the night
As cattle hover near to Him—
This Holy Child of Bethlehem.

Protect Him from the dark'ning deep
And guard Him in His peaceful sleep
In humble manger where He lies—
Out there! A star in eastern skies

That guides the Magi to this place
Where sleeps a child of boundless grace,
A gift from God to all on earth—
This Holy Child of lowly birth.

Mary! Mary! Do hold Him tight.
He is The Way! He is The Light!

Waste Not The Golden Hours

I love the early morning time
When the faint world, serenely still,
Surrounds me with its unlit face,
Then allows the sun's glow to spill
Upon the eastern skies abroad
In scattered streaks of shattered gold.
I know it's time that I should rise
To watch my new morning unfold.

Of a sudden things spring to life:
A sparkle with hope in the air.
With firm avowal of purpose
I have not a moment to spare
Lest I lose my golden chances
To make something of this rare day:
This day The Lord has given me . . .
No! I dare not squander away.

The Promise Of A Rainbow

A rainbow arcs upon a misty sky;
The world below appears to be at peace;
And scudding clouds race to horizon's end.
The brief storm is over; now sweet surcease.

God's promises painted by softened hues,
While whispered zephyrs cool an anxious brow.
These rays of hope upon the thirsting earth—
Nature's way, always Nature's way somehow.

I stand alone in the uplifting calm
In awe of the splendor I have just seen:
God's hands at work on the canvas above.
I'm reassured what his promises mean.

And when a raging storm has passed me by,
God's promise there: a rainbow in the sky.

Reflection

In the early morning hours when I am up
and about before the rising sun,
I relish each softened moment of this very
special time when I may reflect
Upon the blessings of the prior day and others
I am about to receive.
Life is good in the caretaking of our Dear Lord
Who provides everything to us,
And Who nurtures our spirit's needs and
comforts us when we are down and out and sad.

As a mere child I was taught that He was the
answer to all things, and as the one
Who constantly required a push or a shove to
be about, and toil, and perfect
I was prone to be lazy, an idler thinking of many
ways I could deceive
And engage in the hurly-burly of chaos, create a
scene, create a fuss,
Or pretend that everything was in fine order,
job well done as praise made me glad.

But in the scheme of things I am still that child
tending to ignore His wondrous gift:
Salvation offered free, for the taking within the
grasp of just one small prayer;
True bounties of blessings He will share,
comforting my feeble spirit to uplift.
As this child searching for the perfection of all things,
I trust that He is still there.

The Gift Of Faith

Faith is my gift; I know it is.
It glows throughout the darkest day;
It comes from Him; I know it's His,
A beacon's light to show my way.

From the beginning He saved me,
And trusting Him I became whole.
His gift? He gave upon that tree;
Trusting God, He played his role.

Through the Spirit my faith grows strong,
Not my own doing, I am sure.
My heart sings forth in wondrous song;
My soul is cleansed, now white and pure.

In belief of truth I'm set free;
I store my faith within my heart.
He sought me out, and He found me;
And on that day . . . my feeble start.

And I praise Him both day and night.
He is my Way; He is my Light.

The Balm Of Gilead

Is there no balm in Gilead?
Is there no physician there?
Lord, my poor soul is hurting bad.
Do hear my humble prayer.

In times of need I call on You,
And I should praise You even now.
Lord, Oh Lord bring skies of blue,
And lighten my load somehow.

Touch me with the balm I crave
To ease my burden's load.
Rescue me as old Satan's slave,
And send me on down the road.

(Jeremiah 8:22)

To Drink In His Love

I cannot imagine how I've made it
To this juncture in my life without love.
Oh, I do not mean the romantic kind;
I mean His Love that streams from high above.

Three score and ten have simply passed me by
As I crawled and scratched and picked myself up
To reach high plateaus only to fall down
And be forced to drink bitter potion's cup.

What rankles me now is I could have had
His Plan of Salvation at no cost . . . free!
But no! My arrogance held a tight rein,
And I ignored that He died just for me.

So now I drink from the bitterest cup
As I seek intercession from above.
But this awful draught He graciously takes
And gives me a full portion of His Love.

So Easy To Trust Him

Sometimes the burdens of our day
Beset us with their thorns of pain,
And we are prone to run away,
Hoping not to face them again.

Upon a sparkling brand-new day
We rise to greet a splendored sun,
Before us then in grand array
There they are again . . . every one.

The moral to this story is:
Face your troubles as they appear,
Give them to Christ, and they'll be His.
He'll free you from all angst and fear.

How easy, easy to trust Him!
So sure is His Way and His Light !
And should your days suddenly dim,
He's there for you . . . within your sight.

Your Open Door

In the midst of tribulations
I am wont to call on You;
Your door's always open, Dear Lord,
So my words just pass on through.

I know You sift each one of them,
Separate the chaff from wheat.
And when the time is perfect, Lord,
Your answer returns complete.

Many times I hesitated
To call upon You in prayer;
I never believed You would hear me,
Or even that You would care.

But now my heart fills with gladness
Each time that I speak to You;
My words come easy as I talk,
And I know You'll pull me through.

Special Times To Pray

At eventide when set of sun
Strikes rosy time of day,
When shattered skies explode, depart . . .
This is my time to pray.

I thank Him for so many gifts;
Among them there is love,
Cherished friends and food and raiment,
My future home above.

Salvation's Gift He offered us
That day upon the tree;
And all we have to do is ask!
He'll grant it outright . . . free!

At morning's mist when I awake,
My world so soft, aglow;
The clouds of white touch azure skies
Beyond the world I know.

And I am thankful once again,
Taking some time to pray.
Rosy evening or soft morning . . .
Both special times of day.

Reflect, Consider, And Accept

Reflect upon that darkened sky;
Reflect upon Golgotha's tree.
And ask the questions: "Why, God? Why?"
"Thy Will be done!" His painful plea.

Consider that he died that day;
Consider that He walked that road.
Scourged and beaten along that way,
He bore my sins. Such heavy load!

Accept His Gift. It's free! It's free!
Accept His Cross of Calvary!
Then kneel before Him as you pray,
And thank him for that awful day.

Reflect, consider and accept
The full promise that He has kept:
And offer thanks a thousand ways,
Then share His Gift in joyful praise.

The Final Prize

I have a prize awaiting me
Far beyond the distant sky.
And best of all . . . that prize is free,
And someday there I shall fly.

Stronger my faith as I await
Grandest gift Christ offers me.
Everything promised to this date?
Guaranteed at Calvary.

If I stumble along the way,
I'm sure He will pick me up.
I wish to claim my prize one day
And cherish Christ's trophy cup.

"What is this trophy?" one may ask.
I'll say: "Salvation's reward!"
To win that race? Hardly a task,
Obeying God's Holy Word.

There Is No Distinction

We all have sinned and fallen short
But are justified by God's Grace.
A gift it is in all regards
Through redemption's forgiving face.

Led are we by His steady hand
And guided by His warming love.
These, too, are added gifts from him
Abundantly sent from above.

Through Christ we receive wondrous gifts
In full measures that fill each soul;
Though plagued by sin and Satan's pull,
Christ's forgiving touch makes us whole.

(Romans 3:22-24)

Listen And Commit

God works for the good of those who love Him;
Of this much we must be assured.
In suffering, submitting to His Will,
We'll overcome if we've endured

By placing our pains and persecutions,
An act of our personal will;
No need for any of us to suffer
As we ascend life's steepest hill.

Alone, and in doubt none of us should be,
His crystal message loud and clear.
We know He gives His divine direction,
And foremost to all He is near.

It's easy! Listen to His Word.
It's easy! Commit to The Lord.

Solace At Evening

I come to You in the evening
As the sun fades slowly away.
Westward I look, and I'm thinking
Of the words to You I will pray.

Right at first all words evade me,
In vain I struggle with my prayer.
I gaze at the sun's majesty,
Sensing that You are really there.

Then calmness washes over me,
And words come forth in loving praise.
You are My Lord, the King of Kings,
Solace for all my earthly days.

And then arrives a vast darkness
As to my abode I now go;
Safe and secure in my cottage
As the sun sets in pinkish glow.

Rock Me In Your Cradle, Lord

Lord, rock me in Your cradle now;
Rock me gently until I sleep.
And sing the Psalms of David low
That he sang to his grazing sheep.

Lord, tuck me in and comfort me;
Assure me that my heart is right.
Touch my soul with Your nail-scarred hand
That I may sleep through the long night.

And Lord, when the morning breaks fair,
And my night of rest is all done,
I'll give praise to You, Dearest Lord
For sending Christ, Your only Son.

Why Me, Lord?

I know I should not question why
My life has turned out like it is,
For God made me in His image,
And indeed, I am truly His.

But sometimes the doubts do linger
And threaten the peace I have gained.
Weakling that I am, I whimper
As my disposition grows pained.

But then a bright ray of sunshine
Erases my deep sense of loss,
And I am thankful for my Lord
Who sacrificed all on that cross.

So now I never question why
But accept The Lord as He is.
I am truly a child of God,
And indeed, I am truly His.

Questions Unasked

While fleeting shadows from a cloud adrift
Mask brightness from a primal setting sun,
Odd scenes of soft loveliness brashly swift
Plunge out of sight in a much-splendored run.

Rapt, I am there staring into faint space,
Picturing worlds that may have thrived before;
Sensing perforce the structure of each face
And Who shall steer that sun to destined shore.

But old shadows recur as time flies by,
Each dimming the beauty far, far below.
Yet I view gracefulness in patterned sky
And watch with thankful heart the dwindling glow.

The need to be . . . The need to touch the sky . . .
The age-old questions: 'Who?' 'What?' 'Where?'
'When?' 'Why?'

No Need To Ask

If I had three wishes I'd wish for love.
Granted, that may be a selfish demand.
But with such rare things in Heaven above,
I think the Good Lord would lend me a hand.

I don't think I'd ever dare ask for wealth,
For that would be way too greedy, indeed.
I'd pause for a moment, then ask for health.
Granted, that rates as benefit I need.

Thirdly, I'd ask for a long span of years.
But wouldn't that be self-serving of me?
What life He bestows with laughter and tears
I'll savor it, bowing to His Decree.

I'm grateful for every blessing He brings.
And pleased I don't have to ask for these things.

That We Should Give Thanks

I wish to take a moment at each meal
To give thanks for the blessings come my way;
Your kindest touch I always seem to feel;
The precious gift of life for one more day.

And Lord, I dare not forget such good health
(The vim and vigor You have given me.)
And gifts of friendships more valued than wealth,
And surely I can't omit: "I am free!"

Before us now the plenty we shall share:
Full provender that You have sent our way.
Our knowing full well that indeed You care,
And last but not least: lead us forth each day.

A thousand times I've proffered thanks to You
For blessings never-ever overdue.

Oh Ye Of Little Faith!

`Tis but a mustard seed, a grain of sand,
A blazing sky of sun, a night of cold;
An infant's mouth to feed, events unplanned,
A place to hide as destinies unfold.

Quaint scenes from days gone by, a song I know,
A ship to sail away, a note to write;
An apple red or green, a drift of snow,
These all bode well as comes the darkened night.

But a lifetime of love, a wrinkled face,
And I am guided as He surely planned;
The streaking stars above, each one in place,
Move eternally with nudge of His hand.

To be a grain of sand, a minor part,
Marks the leap of faith of a trusting heart.

The Grace That Came To Bear

Christ suffered on that rugged cross.
He gave His life for me.
The shame and suffering that day
And, too, His final plea

For God to take that bitter cup,
And then "Thy Will be done."
But oh, the grace that came to bear
From Him, God's Holy Son.

Redemption of the highest form
Composed upon that day;
My sins, each one, all totaled up
And fully washed away.

And so I live in gratitude
Of sacrifice Christ made.
Hopes for a grand eternal life
Now vividly arrayed.

"Why Have You Forsaken Me?"

"Eloi, Eloi, lema sabachthani?"
At three in the afternoon Jesus cried.
And then the darkness of the day bore out
The dreadful news that Our Lord had then died.

"My God, my God, why have You forsaken me?"
His plaintive voice upon the winds of time.
And soldiers cast lots for his spare clothing
After witnessing the horrific crime.

But what a gift He brought to us that day!
Salvation wrapped in His blood, tears, and sweat.
Eternal life within His Precious Sight . . .
A rare gift available even yet.

In Remembrance

Remember the journey He made;
Remember the arduous road;
Remember the taunts and the jeers;
Remember His burdensome load.

Remember the beatings He took;
Remember the cross that He bore;
Remember His walk up that hill;
Remember the thorns that He wore.

Remember His grand sacrifice;
Remember the blood that He shed;
Remember the gift that He gave;
Remember He rose from the dead.

Remember that He died for you;
Remember that He died for me;
Remember that He will greet us
One day soon in eternity.

The Art Of Worship

I love to hear the words of cheer,
A message each one brings
To tell me that You're ever near,
For then my sad heart sings.

I love to see the skies of blue
That greet each precious day;
I waken then and talk to You;
My favorite time to pray.

Oh! I'm happy and of good cheer.
Your blessings fill my heart;
And the notes come forth – Oh, so clear!
A beauty they impart.

And when the evening shadows fall,
I speak to You once more.
I praise You for the day You've made,
Tomorrows yet in store.

Remembrance

Remembrance of a time ago
When Christ walked that rocky road
And lugged that cross of rugged hew,
And carried our sinful load.

Remembrance of His anguish then
When he heard the taunts and jeers
Of the very souls He would save
From death and their unknown fears.

Remembrance of the last few steps
When He stood there with one thought,
And carried out God's ordered plan,
Our mortal sins had He bought.

Remembrance of His dying breath
When He gave His life for me:
And then the darkened clouds rolled in;
All mankind from sin was free.

The Perfect Power Of Prayer

A little prayer at eventide,
An orison at morn's sun;
Patiently Christ stands by my side
When my day is over and done.
So thankful for His presence, I
Lift up my heart in praise.
My prayer now wafts to Him on high
Beyond His endless days.

So sweet it is to talk in peace.
He hears my every plea.
Each gift of His offers sweet surcease;
That's what prayer was meant to be.

Perfection: His timing, I know;
Perfection: His receptive heart,
Attuned to my own ebb and flow,
He's been hearing me from the start.

Within My Faith

If I should lapse within my faith,
I ask to have enough
To turn the tide of temptations.
At times that can be tough.

As a true bulwark of my faith,
Indeed, He's at my side
Nudging, pushing me on my path,
Quelling my sinful pride.

I am wont to remind myself:
Salvation's gift is free.
His anguished suffering that day—
Long hours on Calvary.

And when I fail to meet the test,
I'm shamed beyond belief.
For He picked me up and touched me
And gave me sweet relief.

To Lose Oneself

What profit does it gain a man
Amassing fortunes untold,
To lose them when he leaves this earth,
These hoards of silver and gold?

Cold comfort for the life he's led,
Each unmoving shiny thing;
For within dark casket he must lie,
Never to gain one more spring.

Upon this earth he paid no heed,
Too busy with his career;
Nature's beauty surrounding him
Limned vacuous and unclear.

Then in the flash of a moment,
His life played out scene-by-scene.
All treasures lost, no recompense—
His prospects now slim and mean.

And so his profits netted him
But naught in his stressful years;
For losing them he lost himself
As he neared his vale of tears.

The Master Eraser

Upon a day when I may doubt,
I ask The Lord to clear my mind,
Erasing all my troubling thoughts,
And leaving all my doubts behind.

Christ is The Master Eraser:
His precious blood shed on that day,
Removing all aspects of doubt
And washing all my sins away.

I feel remiss when I may doubt
For the picture is vivid, clear.
I'm but a blackboard in this life
With Christ and His Eraser near.

Not Where You Start

It's not where you start; it's where you finish.
In Bethlehem our Dear Savior began
His fated trek on earth destined by God.
Every step, every word part of God's Plan.

'Where do I start?' I often ask myself.
'What does my Savior have in store for me?'
'Why should I bother with such things as these?'
For when Christ died on the cross, I was free.

The day I was born I started my trek,
Arrogant and sinful in many ways.
Then I found Christ; the *real* journey began.
Gladly I'll finish it one of these days.

Quietude

In prayer there comes a quietude,
A softened moment when
One talks to God in solitude
And feels so special then

Possessing God's Ear one-on-one,
Letting one's anguish out,
Resting within the Spirit's zone,
To cast away each doubt.

Oh, this is bliss in humble pose,
To worship Him above;
I do it often, I suppose,
To gain His undying love.

Within His Great Love

Within my heart I wish to know
My Savior's Plan for me.
I'll pray each day, my faith will grow;
His Grace will set me free.

Within the bounds of His Great Love
My heart now fills with pride
To know He watches from above
And bids me to abide.

Within the reach of nail-scarred hand,
Reminder of the cross;
One touch from Him; I understand
True meaning of that loss.

Within my soul now white and pure,
Forgiven of sins am I;
For now I live and shall endure
To know the reasons why

Within my heart a great love flows
Each hour of the day.
My Savior cares; my Savior knows;
My Savior leads the way.

Where Lilies Bloom

Where lilies bloom I wish to go
To see the fair beauty of
Their petals in their skyward thrust:
Rare picture of His Pure Love.

The Lily of the Valley, He,
And the Bright and Morning Star;
His lilies, symbols of His Love,
Accept us just as we are.

And then one day in Heaven soon
Fair lilies will I attend
In fields of glowing bright on bright:
A view I can recommend.

So Thankful . . .

So thankful for the Lamb of God
Who gave His Life to free
The world of sin from Satan's grasp:
Grand gift for you and me.

A day to live in memory,
Eternally, and then more.
His Sacrifice on that one day?
No hope at all before.

Christ took the burden of our sins,
A package hard to bear,
To give us life for years on end;
I'm thankful He was there.

These Things I Know

Lord, I know You move the mountains
And rattle them until they blow,
The gases flowing like fountains
As You watch each one's ebb and flow.

Lord, I know You push the oceans
In tidal explosions apace,
And rein in their errant motions
As eastward/westward they all race.

Lord, I know You paint the sky blue,
Its azure tinting far and deep,
Its vastness known only to You . . .
(A hushed secret You plan to keep.)

Lord, I know You gave Your life there
On that stark cross at Calvary;
You struggled up that hill to where
All of mankind would be set free.

Lord, I cannot fathom Your pain,
All the suffering You endured.
I know You'd do it all again
If salvation were not assured.

This Journey I Have Taken

A journey here I have taken
Divined and prescribed I know
By a loving God Who made me,
The same as the fallen snow.

Actions and steps I have taken
Were determined long ago
By a loving God Who loved me,
Or else this could not be so.

I have stumbled along the way,
Often wand'ring to and fro;
But God offers a Helping Hand
To lead me where I should go.

And now my journey nears its end.
I shall reap what I have sown.
I have no fear for He's still near:
Precious God I've always known.

Echoes Of The Heart

The chords now echo from my heart;
I sing the songs I hear
And parlay these to symphonies
To sate my spirit's ear.

For I am wont to strike new notes
And never know just why
The bars and measures seem to please
My own discerning eye.

I touch the strings in fretted pose
To let the sounds depart,
And there I hear a velvet voice—
It is my silent heart.

Finding Home

This is the place that I call home;
This is the place where I
Once looked beyond the stars above
And sought a perfect sky;

And found it not until that time
I knew the meaning of
Reality which thus ensued
And showed me God's True Love.

Imprints

A central hope in living is
The thought that lets me know
My steps in life are like bold tracks
Imprinted on the snow;

That with a melting clarity
Once led to days ahead,
Recording hesitations of
The life that I had led;

But disappeared into cold mists
With countless others, and
Then left the faintest vestiges
On this well-traveled land;

I pray to God that of my steps
Imprinted, set apart,
That more than one shall blaze a trail,
Show others where to start;

For in the core of my own prayer
The theme shall let me know:
The steps I've made shall leave sure prints
Though comes new-fallen snow.

Indeed!

He touches me with nail-scarred hands
To make my spirit whole;
A cherished touch of Heaven's Grace—
He calms my tortured soul;

What brings to bear this gift to share
Is Christ The Risen Lord
Who gave His life: the greatest gift—
And thus such sweet accord.

I could not live without His touch,
Without His constant care;
He is the whole of who I am—
The answer to my prayers.

How vibrant this His healing touch
Upon one's pressing need;
A blessed gift – in purest form—
Indeed! Indeed! Indeed!

Commitment: And I Shall Go . . .

If He should call me, I shall go
To edge of night in depths of snow;
In noonday sun, in evening shade,
In dappled light of forest glade.

If He should call me, I shall hear
His calming voice; I bear no fear;
He beckons me to follow Him
On star-filled nights, on pathways dim.

If He should call me, I shall trust;
My faith grows stronger, as it must;
He is the Light; He is the Way,
The Only Hope for one more day.

And when He calls me, I shall know—
And I shall go; and I shall go.

Just One More Gift

Grant me the gift of patience, Lord;
A thimbleful have I;
Fill my heart with its plenitude:
My wish before I die.

Grant me the gift of empathy;
In others' shoes I'll walk;
And still my tongue if it grows sharp;
Subdue its careless talk.

I dare not ask for any more,
My Dearest Lord above;
But if You send just one more gift,
Send me the Gift of Love.

From That One Seed

Do give us hope; lend us a hand;
Nudge us along; we understand
That faith grows like a mustard seed
Planted with love by one good deed.

We're thankful for Your helping hand;
Our needless fears You countermand
By blooms of faith from that one seed—
For that is all, Dear Lord, we need.

A Touch Of Grace

In me there dwells a touch of grace;
I feel it in my soul—
A throbbing essence I've attained
To make my being whole.

Without His Sacred Bounty I
Must fail as claimant to
His Promise of Eternal Life—
Though He will see me through.

His Grace does bide invisible,
As benison it lives;
All hearts restored to purity
By Grace, as God forgives.

Always There

So often have I come to You
To lay my conscience bare;
At any time, at any place,
I always find You there:
In chapel hushed, in humble room,
Wherever I might pray;
I only had to come to You—
You somehow showed the way.

I think today I'll talk to You,
Speak only of those things
With which You bless me every day;
Vast joy each one brings.
Tomorrow I shall come to you
To worship You with praise;
I'll always find You there, I know;
For endless are Your Days.

And should I live a hundred years
Or perish ere the dawn—
At any time, at any place,
I'll find You on my own.

**Then said Jesus unto his disciples,
"If any man will come after me, let him deny
Himself, and take up his cross, and follow me."**

(King James Version, The Holy Bible)

For In A Moment

In anguish do I call upon
The Lord to beg relief;
No obstacle in starchy pose
Can thwart my true belief;
For in a moment clarified
His words come to my ears;
And I, no longer filled with angst,
Dismiss unfounded fears.

Awaiting An Invitation

If I should place a value on
The things I have at hand,
So little I would have to rate—
Not much at my command.

My treasures few, my money spare,
My savings all but nil;
A rented cottage I call home—
No mansion on a hill.

So with great faith I travel on
To meet each wondrous day;
And thank the Lord for what I have—
Then go my humble way.

Complainer I? No way, indeed!
My treasures all laid by;
For I await my welcome to
His mansions in the sky.

His Thread Of Life

Today's a time that could not be
Had not one day ago
His Thread of Life extended to
A future I could know
In which the sun in westward flight
Sought out another day
To break upon that which was dark
With thrust of shining ray.

And thus He comes, so like the sun,
Extending life unto
Today, tomorrow and beyond—
His Promise shining through.
And I am part and parcel of
A time He meant to be;
Today? His Gift, His Thread of Life—
A future offered me.

A Matter Of Faith

Faith is that spark within our souls
That sets the heart aglow,
Believing things that are not seen,
Some things we cannot know.

But trust within us offers hope—
That flint to start a fire;
To see those things that are not seen
To which our hearts aspire.

I sense that spark each given day;
And as my faith grows stronger still
That tiny light now guides my way:
I see those things and know His Will.

Ever-present Is He

There comes a time within each life
When troubles rule the day;
And in the clutch of circumstance
All hope seems swept away.

The world turns black at evening sun
As shadows bring on night.
Bereft, it seems, one's shattered soul
As hope has taken flight.

For in the drawn-out hours ahead
Each minute's misery
Returns in time to morning's glow;
Then hope embraces me.

Indeed, He is my morning's light,
Yet He was there throughout my night.

Splendid Expectations

Before the sunrise breaks upon
The eastern skies that hold
The scattered shards of yesterday
In cache of melted gold,
I am awake and waiting for
The hint of His surprise—
That streaking shaft of carmine's touch
To tease expectant eyes;

And in a moment too supreme
My spirits soar to heights
Beyond the bounds I'd not demand
On morning's vast delights;
Again, once more, anew, afresh—
I view my new-found day
And know full well that God has made
This splendid disarray.

The Rarest Gem

The gift of life,
Rare gem indeed . . .
Bestowed upon
The Common Herd;
But in man's heart
A blazing need
To be . . . To be!

Positively

Within my world of happiness
I make my spirit glad
By thinking of all positives,
Not problems I have had.

Too short my life; too brief the hours
To idly fret away.
Full I live in His Here and Now
With each new gilded day.

Tenfold

Love will not find you; it is blind,
Its eyes closed to the endless quest;
And should it by mere happenstance
Find you, let it be; let it rest.

Love will not find you, seek you out,
Its heart steeled to the journey's goal;
And should it by a luckless step
Find you, let it embrace your soul.

Love will not find you, though it lives
In hearts and souls of all good men;
But should you find it, hold it fast—
A priceless treasure ten times ten.

On Pedestals Of Equity

Love knows no color as does hate;
Love reaches out in darkest night;
Love holds a hand of unknown hue;
Love comforts whether black or white.
Love does not question, nor does it
Discern one's shade before embrace;
Love brings concern for one's true plight,
Ignoring color of one's face.

Love knows no bounds, no limits to
Its focus on one's soul within;
Inclusive in His Heart of Hearts,
Ignoring color of one's skin.
Love is not love if it excludes;
Love must, in fact, place one and all
On equity's true pedestals—
As sacred duty to His Call.

The Ultimate Gift

New valleys green; old hills grown soft
From skies of blue; white clouds aloft
Which make their way to edge of night—
My thanks to God for gift of sight.

The years that He shall give to me
All His beauty I could not see—
Too vast, too deep, to no surprise,
Grandeur untold shall miss my eyes;

And I shall be the lesser for
The unseen valleys, soft hills or
Pursuing clouds to edge of night—
But oh the beauty and delight

Of dreaming of the things I'll see
When all His gifts are given me;
When I shall shatter bonds of night
To stand rewarded in His sight.

Reborn By Trust

How green it was a time ago,
But now the sheen is gone;
It was a time that I loved so
On which old suns had shone

And brought a luster to the scene
That met my eyes each day;
It was a time of splendid green
That now has slipped away;

But it will come; I know it must
As part and parcel of
A time reborn by my own trust:
This spring of God's Pure Love.

The Wonder Of

I find the greatest joy in
The old, familiar things;
To think of them as they once were,
Such pleasure each now brings.

The essence of rare friendship that
Has lasted through the years;
The time once spent in happiness
Offsetting trying tears.

The smiling eyes, a thoughtful brow,
The look on caring face;
Naiveté of children who
Seem blessed with God's True Grace.

I find great reassurance in
So many wondrous things;
And as I cite them, one by one,
My heart forever sings.

Unto His Radiance

What strengthened thread holds life and limb
And sinew to the bone?
What pulses to a heart, a soul,
On which no light has shone?
What gives unto His Radiance
Like butterfly on high,
Which in a ray of sunshine must
Perforce begin to fly?

What deed of trust unrecognized,
Unwritten though it be,
Creates an atom's inner core?
A life's first energy?
What acts of fate, what answers to
All subtle questions asked,
Lead to His Grace and Radiance
In which each life has basked?

Unto the depth and breadth of time—
Unto my life and limb—
Unto the pulsing of my heart—
I owe my soul to Him.

To Go Back Home

How very hard to go back home,
For that is where one's heart
Once brimmed with songs of happiness
And made its token start.

How difficult to go back there
To places in one's mind,
Which in a caution may arouse
Old things which prove unkind.

Before the lapse of memories
One's psyche moves to mend
A broken heart, a troubled mind,
Made whole before the end.

How easy then to go back home
To places in one's soul
Which mix and mesh and come to terms
And make one's spirit whole.

Somewhere An Answer

Somewhere out there an answer that
We lowly men pursue;
We peer beyond the blackened stars,
Yet have nor hint nor clue

Of what has been, or what shall be,
Or what the answer is;
Through stellar depths, through airless flight—
All time, all space are His.

In reckoning, in probing for,
The dusts from ill-born flame,
His magnitude of universe
Must glorify His name;

And we, mere speck of nothingness,
Asea in our poor flight,
Do what we do as we should do,
Admitting His Great Might.

Somewhere out there an answer that
We lowly men pursue;
We soar beyond our nothingness
And find the answer: Who.

The Joy Of His Gifts

I think that I shall bide my time
To dwell upon a thought
That He has given me today—
A lesson to be taught.

A golden sun to light my day,
A moon to glow at night;
A rainbow when a storm must fade
Assuring all is right.

And shooting stars across His Sky
As on and on they go;
The seasons of a passing year:
Penultimate comes snow.

So many things to dwell upon,
Each one a treasured gift;
I praise Him for His Loving Care
And Blessings that uplift.

Waiting

In fact and deed a faith have I,
Unbounded I can tell;
My visions reach to edge of time—
I know that all is well;

My bedrock based on granite's clasp,
Assurance ever mine;
From east to west and north to south
My days will be just fine;

And in the future years, I know,
I'll gain a welcomed rest;
And I shall look beyond His stars—
For there will be His best.

A Tiny Dot

Near ocean's edge I watch the waves
Slowly draw near in destined aim.
They foam to cover lifeless forms
Long, long succumbed to nature's claim.

In endless reach the ocean's realm,
Boundless its miles in massive pose.
While standing there I feel quite small:
The merest dot, I would suppose.

But in my heart I know He knows:
Omniscient God of all mankind.
He sees me now—a tiny dot—
And should I go astray, I'll find

That He stands there on sinking sands
Rescuing me with outstretched hands.

Always, Always . . .

I wish you enough of all good things;
And I wish you wondrous golden days.
I wish you a robin red that sings;
And I wish you these . . . always, always.

I wish you an infant dear that clings;
And I wish you splendor's sunset rays.
I wish you a golden bell that rings;
And I wish you these . . . always, always.

I wish you a love to rouse your heart;
And I wish you wondrous golden days.
I wish you a place where you may start;
And I wish you these . . . always, always.

I wish you peace as the end draws near;
And I wish you splendor's sunset rays.
I wish you freedom from all dark fear;
And I wish you these . . . always, always.

My Personal GPS

I know so little of technical stuff;
I'm a dinosaur, so they say.
But I have a marvelous Pathfinder!
And all I have to do is pray.

Navigation, precision aren't my bag;
I get lost several times each day.
All I have to do is look heavenward!
And He graciously leads the way.

What is this Marvel that I must possess?
I, old dinosaur, as they say?
A God-given tool for sinners like me!
And all I have to do is pray.

Androids, robotics: exotic things,
All true marvels in their own way.
But I don't really need any of them!
For all I have to do is pray.

God's GPS is unfailing for me;
No batteries, wires everywhere.
His ever-present arms always open!
His Light shines as I kneel in prayer.

And Come Those Days

And come those days when I am sad and blue,
A bit despondent about many things.
But I brace up and remind myself Who
Can send me a robin that trills and sings

The songs of the happiest springtime day,
When the waft of fragrances fills the air,
When the sun is pleasantly warm in May;
Everything I see gleams without compare.

I have no idea why I was sad,
Or despondent in such a pretty place;
Soft surroundings should comfort, make me glad,
And I should be thankful for God's True Grace.

And so I go about each daily chore,
Happy in my newfound state I now thrive;
And breathing quite deeply I savor more
As the heart and soul of me come alive.

Just A Few Requests, Lord

Lord, shine Your Light upon my face
And bring Your Spirit to bear;
And by Your Guidance and Your Grace
Walk beside me everywhere.

And send Your Blessings one by one
When I trip and fall so low;
When I'm bereft and feel alone,
Direct me where I should go.

Teach me, Lord, how I should pray
Those moments I talk to You.
You are The Light; You are the Way,
The Only One Who is true.

And when at last I see Your Face
And view Your Radiant Glow,
I'll know Your Guidance and Your Grace
By salvation You'll bestow.

I Wish You Enough

When days grow short and nights stretch long,
And doubts prevent a restful sleep,
Lift up your heart in praiseful song,
Surrender to the Master's Keep.

When burdens of a tiresome day
Encompass you and vex your soul,
Lift up your heart and simply pray:
"Dear Lord, I'm yours. Please make me whole."

And as the days go slowly by,
Protracted seem the golden years,
Lift up your heart and let it fly
To soar above life's taxing fears.

And when your work on earth is done,
Your victory assured, so tough,
I wish you naught but golden sun;
And lastly? I wish you enough.

Finding Faith

Within my heart I know He's there.
I sense a peace unto my soul.
It is a blessing. Oh, so rare!
Indeed, I feel as if I'm whole.

Before He came into my heart
My life spiraled out of control.
Rejecting Him, I wished no part,
So arrogant was my sinful role.

So rough was I around my edge,
I gave no thought to Christ at all.
I spurned religion as a wedge
Against His Message and His Call.

I knew nothing of faith or love,
Nor things hoped for each dawning day;
Nor evidence of God above . . .
Quite frankly, I had lost my way.

But then a dear friend took my hand,
And Christ came through my once-closed door.
Now I have faith. I understand
Christ's message of faith, love and more.

A Quiet Orison

I send a whisper on the wind
Whether it be full day or night;
And softly comes His healing balm:
His nail-scarred hands with touch so light.

I'm lifted up before I fall
As He accompanies me in stride;
My heart is warmed; my soul is thrilled,
Knowing He's with me at my side.

No vocal answer do I need
When I send up my plaintive plea;
His nail-scarred hands have reassured
And bring a great solace to me.

It matters not to our Dear Lord
Whether it be daytime or night,
A few words sent as simple prayer
And everything will be all right.

His Way Of Sadness

It was His way of sadness, and
It was His path of grief.
Pebbles, rocks and sinking sand;
Jesus found no sweet relief.

Up, up He strove to that vile hill;
He stumbled in His pace.
The soldiers lashed Him with brutes' will;
His blood ran down His face.

The cross He bore for you and me?
It chafed His Spirit sore.
A few more steps to Calvary
With the crown of thorns He wore.

One hammered nail into His hand . . .
The taunts and jeers rang out . . .
And then another by command . . .
And a soldier gave a shout.

And on that cross He died that way,
Oh! Suffering woefully!
But what a gift He brought that day:
Eternal life for you and me.

Before His Sacrifice

No guarantees before Christ gave
His Life upon that tree;
For each was naught but Satan's slave
Until He set us free.

Salvation's gift Christ gave to all
As on His dying breath,
He prayed to God, His final call:
"Thy Will be done!", then death.

The Savior of all mortal men
Then drew a guttered breath.
And lo! A darkness settled in;
An old world saw its death.

And we were free, so free at last
To reap full blessings of
Forgiveness of our sins long passed,
Then bask in His Pure Love.

Heaven's Bounty

Consider a rainbow's splendored hues;
Consider a mountain's snowcapped crest;
Consider a child on mother's knee;
And you have truth at its very best.

Look upon an early morning's dew;
Look upon a golden sun gone west;
Look upon a hummingbird in flight;
And you have seen beauty at its best.

Hold a tiny baby in your hands;
Hold a dear old friend close to your breast;
Hold no grudges as you go through life;
And you have sensed pure love at its best.

Consider, look and hold onto these
With delight: Truth, beauty and pure love.
Each one will bring great blessings to you
To share from Heaven's bounty above.

In Praiseful Submission

Dear Lord, I thank You for the dawn
(Another splendored day);
Blue skies, white clouds to look upon
In riotous array.

A misty sheen upon the lawn
Like diamonds in the dew;
Soft whisper of a breeze upon
These gifts, indeed, from You.

Your seasons come; Your seasons go,
Each one so planned by You.
And at each time I surely know
That nothing's overdue.

And when the end of day draws near,
I take a moment to
Unload my doubt, toss out my fear,
Submit myself to You.

A Saving Grace

Abiding in my heart today:
Sanctification by His Grace.
It is the route, the only way
To meet Him face-to-face.

Before Christ came to save mankind
On that lowly Golgotha tree,
Approach to God was law-defined:
Salvation hardly free.

When Christ shed His Blood for us all
On that starkest, most awful day,
He bade God's Bidding and His Call
To wash man's sins away.

And so I savor His Grace now
As I stumble through each new day.
Sensing His Presence, I somehow
Find His Light and His Way.

Always Good To Me

I'm thankful for so many things,
But remiss I tend to be
In gratefulness for His blessings,
For He's always good to me.

I tot them up: so many gifts
In graciousness He will share.
There's life and home: each one uplifts;
Food and raiment beyond compare.

And health awarded each new day
To make my low spirits soar;
And sunshine in its golden ray.
Dear friend, dare I ask for more?

Yes! Salvation's most wondrous prize
He gave that day on the Cross;
Within that promised premise lies
Eternal life through His loss.

And shame should rest upon me now
Should I not praise Him in prayer;
He's always good to me somehow,
In my need He's always there.

Always And Ever

His is my Savior; my Relief
Who steals my heart and soul each night,
Who in the dark unlike a thief
Brings joy with the morning light.

Oh, He is more than that I'd say,
A beacon's glow on storm-tossed sea
That guides my ship along the way
To bring me home where I should be.

My Rock of Ages lest I fall,
On Him I shall lean more and more;
He's always present when I call
With blessings bountiful in store.

And I am on a periled flight
Upon the surge of roaring tide,
But He protects me through the night
Always and ever at my side.

Get Thee Behind Me, Satan

When Satan tempts, just hold your ground.
Stand firm and tall and face your foe.
Soon, very soon you will rebound
To tell Satan where he may go.

His offers will seem enduring,
His pictures enormous in scope.
Everything will be alluring:
Promises of riches and hope.

He'll tantalize you with big dreams;
They will loom as epic to you.
With him nothing is what it seems;
His falsehoods will never ring true.

The solution to all of this is
To tell him to go straight to Hell.
A Child of God? You can't be His.
I know this far better than well.

He's Always Near

Somehow I sense when He is near;
A warmness glows within my heart.
And I am free of doubts and fear,
These things a world apart.

Somehow I hear a gentle voice;
It lets me know that He is near.
And I feel comfort and rejoice,
And know He'll reappear.

Somehow I've learned to talk to Him;
I say a very simple prayer.
And I am drawn to Bethlehem.
Yes! To a manger there.

Somehow I know He came to give
His life upon that cruel tree.
Because of that I know I'll live
With Him eternally.

Bring Me Peace, Oh Lord!

Bring me peace, Oh Lord! I cry out to You
In moments of distress when I am blue;
Unhappy times when skies turn ashen gray,
Or when the setting sun closes my day.

Or at morning's light bringing skies of blue,
And I am forlorn, I cry out to You.
Or on troubling days when time speeds away,
Or when the sun fades in fleeting array.

But my cries are wrong, Lord, I should not ask
For a peace before I attempt each task.
In happy times I should proffer a prayer,
So thankful to know that You're always there.

I should cry out to You in thanksgiving
For all blessings: salvation, forgiving,
Promise of eternal life always there;
And all I have to do is say one prayer.

So simple it is when I cry to You,
But my thanks, Oh Lord, are long overdue.
Now that I have peace, my fears held at bay,
I thank You, Lord, for one more special day.

Faith Defined

What is faith? A tiny mustard seed
That flourishes in a loamy soil?
Then thrives near to a devilish weed
As toward the warming sun it must toil?

What is faith? An acorn 'neath old oak
That must escape the ravenous swine?
And claw its way heavenward or choke
On damp leaves, then sprout in green divine?

What is faith? A tiny grain of sand
That once was part of gigantic stone?
Once tossed about in an Ice Age land,
Now sparkling in a tropical zone?

What is faith? It's more than just these three.
It's trust in Christ and the Spirit too.
And best of all? It is richly free.
Embrace it, and God will see you through.

A Thorn In My Flesh

Preparing to be conceited
Because of great things I was told,
My ego overblown and vain,
My spirit relaxed and gone cold.

A thorn in the flesh given me,
A messenger of Satan's clan,
Torments to begin much too soon . . .
Each a part of The Master's Plan.

Three times I pleaded with The Lord
To take it all away from me;
But in His Wisdom He said "No!"
Emphatic were His words, you see:

"For my power is made perfect;
My grace is sufficient for you,"
I shall boast of my weaknesses
So that Christ's power may ensue.

I delight in my weaknesses,
Insults, hardships, difficulties,
In persecutions from abroad . . .
Then I am strong, strong . . . don't you see?

Sufferings and persecutions
Placed in His loving hands by will,
No one needs to suffer alone;
Commit it to The Lord . . . until.

An Act Of Love

Forgiveness is an act of love,
A cleansing of stained heart
In which old ills are thrown away
To bring on freshened start.

A union of two souls begins
With tide and time reset;
And in a rarefied moment
One says, "Pray, let's forget."

One big smile brings on another
As tears flow from the eyes;
And storm-tossed clouds soon fade away
Reflecting clear blue skies.

The hearts are healed, the souls renewed
As hands are intertwined.
In friendship's love the two become
Of single heart and mind.

A Favor, Lord

A favor, Lord, if I may ask;
If I may trouble You.
This thing called life is quite a task,
So please, Lord, see me through.

Grant me the sunshine's brightest ray
When storm clouds roll about.
Chastise me whenever I stray
If I have left You out.

Bring me all mornings bright and fair,
Evenings with golden light;
And when to bed I do repair,
Protect me through the night.

And at the end when I grow old,
Walk with me as I go.
I need Your Hand; I am less bold;
These things You surely know.

I trust that I have well-served You,
That You've forgiven me.
There are no favors overdue:
In fact, Salvation's free.

I Wish

I wish for you a rainbow's beam
Upon a rain-splashed glade
With colors only God could know
Because these tints He made.

I wish for you an April rain
Upon a thirsty field
With moisture only God could send
Increasing your crop's yield.

I wish for you an azure sky
Upon your homey place
With zephyrs only God could urge
Caressing your fair face.

I wish for you salvation's gift
Upon your sad goodbye
With angels only God could ask
To lift you to His Sky.

I wish for me a chance to go
Upon that fateful day
To see my God and others who
Have helped along the way.

For I'll embrace them one-by-one
And greet them with a smile.
I'll know them all, for they once walked
With me my troubled mile.

I Wish You Mercy, Peace And Love

May mercy, peace and love
Be multiplied to you.
And may the Lord above
Reward with skies of blue.

He'll give us warming sun
To chase a chilly day.
(He sent His Only Son
To Whom we all may pray).

Cool rains to make grass green
When summer suns blaze hot,
And wondrous mountain scenes
In scapes that time forgot.

Soft rainbows to remind
That hope remains in view.
And neighbors who are kind
In thoughtful deeds they do.

And friends who stand by us
When sorrow gets us down;
They help us without fuss,
Their kindness honor-bound.

May mercy, peace and love
Be multiplied to all.
And to the Lord above
We'll heed His duty's call.

Jude 1:2

My Morning Prayers

When eastern skies erupt in golden streaks,
I rise to greet a new and blessed day.
In prayerful thought I thank my Lord above,
For this is my favorite time to pray.

The freshness in the air renews my soul;
The early morning mist falls softly then;
And I exult in all the blessings that
Make me one of the luckiest of men.

God is good, and He resides in my heart.
I'll always proffer Him my morning praise.
Accepting His gift of eternal life,
I'll extol His goodness for all my days.

And one day soon upon a morning's crest
Unto His arms I'll fly to peaceful rest.

Chaff Before The Wind

Let my sins fly far, far away,
Afloat as chaff before the wind.
Cleanse my heart, Lord, and set me free,
To my hopeful prayers please attend.

Rip out rancor surging in me,
Cast it beyond horizon's pale.
And touch the essence of my soul;
For then I'll know that all is well.

I bow to You in prayerful pose,
Accept salvation's wondrous gifts,
Acknowledge You as King of Kings,
Praise Your Presence as it uplifts.

And in the end as time draws near,
I'll hold You close and have no fear.

Psalm 35:5

Lord, Lift Me Up

Lord, grant me peace when I am sad,
And wrap me in your arms of love.
And smile on me when I am glad;
And when it comes to push and shove.

Grant me the courage to stand tall
And face the problems of each day.
And when my back is 'gainst life's wall,
Dear Lord, do hear me as I pray.

Grant me deep love for fellow man;
Teach me the art of empathy.
Lead me to do the things I can
For those adrift on life's cruel sea.

Lift me up with your nail-scarred hands.
You are the One Who understands.

Away With Thee!

"Forsooth!" One dare not say that word today
   Lest he draw the stares of strangers about.
"Egad!" "Gadzooks!" Words no longer in play,
   Or "Tally Ho!" heard as a rousing shout.

"Betwixt" a rock and hard place we may be,
   Though these days it's affirmed we're in a jam.
Now courtly swains do not on bended knee
Doff their feathered hats, bow low and say "Ma'am."

"Nay!" The world in which we now live has changed.
   "Prithee," indulge me in my quest for truth.
"Zounds!" We've tweeted, twittered, English
              Deranged;
   So in this world I dare say it: "Forsooth!"

"Mayhap" it shall all turn about once more,
   But "Knowest thou," it pricks my psyche sore.

An Illogical Wish

I'd like to live my life over;
So many things I'd surely do.
I would pause and pick a clover,
And I'd think more often of you.

I'd count the petals one-by-one,
Etching each fond wish in my heart.
Then dwell on those days our sun shone,
Long before we drifted apart.

But wishing does not make it so,
And the past can never be now.
That adage I learned long ago
But had forgotten it somehow.

So in the few days that remain
I'll cherish all whom I call friend.
My past forgotten with its pain,
Bright future that'll never end.

A Word Plain And Simple

I've gained true meaning of a word
That I sought through long years of prayer.
It was a word I seldom heard,
Though I knew it was always there.

I sought it in my carnal way
And for a moment thought I'd be
On top of my world for one day;
But alas! It rejected me.

I found it when I shared my plight
With a dear and most cherished friend.
That word burst forth in shining light,
And my search had come to an end.

What is this one word? I'll tell you.
It is a word that we all need.
The only word in life that's true:
It's "Love" plain and simple, indeed!

Each New Day

Upon a golden morning when
The sun peeks through the haze,
I'm so very blessed to be here,
I pause, take time to praise

The Good Lord Who presents each day,
Rewarding with His gifts.
His sky in azure's hue above,
Grand splendor that uplifts.

But I'm remiss, I am afraid,
Take for granted, you see.
It does not have to be this way,
His vistas always free.

He sends the sun each morning when
The world awakens to
A brand new day to further life,
A time to give Him due.

And so I thank Him for His gifts,
Remiss I shall not be.
One thing I always thank Him for?
Eternal life for me.

I Wish To Remember Christmas

I wish to remember Christmas
As it was so long, long ago—
Bracing rides on a one-horse sleigh
On country lanes covered by snow.

I wish to remember Christmas
And the short jaunt to Grandma's place—
Meals at her big oval table,
All holding hands and saying Grace.

I wish to remember Christmas
With shiny presents neath the tree—
Surprise opening each package
And exclaiming loudly, "For me?"

I wish to remember Christmas
And the message that it imparts—
Lessons we learned about giving
With love warming each of our hearts.

I cherish each precious moment
From those times so long, long ago—
But Christmas is much more than that:
It's about our Savior, you know.

"... And Follow Me"

Three little words so simply put,
So poignant in their scope of love:
"Take up your cross and follow Me."
He is The Gift from God above.

No strong command in these few words
But opportunity to be
Disciples of The Loving Christ:
"Take up thy cross and follow Me."

Had I not heard the last three words
Forlorn and lost I'd surely be;
For Christ suffered His All for us
That anguished day at Calvary.

When I am wont to stray in sin,
I think of these words . . . Yes, all three!
In praise of God and His Pure Love,
I hear Christ's words: "And follow Me!"

He Is My Everything

He lights the Evening Star, I'm told.
He flecks the glint in purest gold.
He beams the Morning Star as well.
He tunes the chiming of a bell.

He strikes the flash in lightning's bolt.
He prodes the dash of lively colt.
He sends a rainbow at storm's end.
He gives His Love—no end! No end!

He cools the moon; He warms the sun.
He bids us happiness and fun.
He drives a comet streaking bright.
He paints the skies on starlit night.

He is The Hope to which I cling.
He is My All, My Everything.
He is My Savior—oh, so dear!
He is Salvation, free and clear.

A Place To Talk

Had I planted the roses then
When first I knelt in prayer
In garden of sweet memories,
They would have flourished there.

Upward, upward they would reach
To touch the sun's warm rays;
Bloom velvet in their quietude
And live for countless days.

Veiled fragrances upon the air,
Each one a perfumed gift,
Refreshing on a weary day,
My spirit to uplift.

And so it is with all my prayers,
When to this garden I go,
I kneel and hand my sins to Him.
Then watch His flowers grow.

Everything

Incredible that He would live
And die, blood running down His Face;
Yet He would say, "Father, forgive!"
Unworthy are we of His Grace.

We can only give thanks and praise
For the mercy He offers free;
Christ is The Essence of our days:
Salvation granted on that tree.

Imperfect are we in all things,
Though our hearts are cleansed by His Blood.
To each table Christ always brings
His News that is forever good.

I am unworthy of you, Lord,
Though I respond, obey and love;
I receive true faith through Your Word,
And one day I'll see You above.

My Grand Choice

How in my plight of circumstance
I lift Him up in prayer!
No iffy odds, no gambler's chance,
For He is ever there

To touch my soul, to ease my heart,
Assuage my inward pain.
And then my worries all depart,
And I am whole again.

How in my night of circumstance
When in a moment, I
Acknowledge Him in prayerful stance.
I'll praise Him 'til I die!

And then in Heaven I'll rejoice
With Him for endless days.
How in the core of my grand choice
I'll sing eternal praise.

Lord, I Love You

Lord, I love You. You know I do.
You're the One who's steady and true.
You chase dark skies with azure blue,
  And when I call for help, it's You.

Lord, I love You each day and night;
  You're the One who's forever right.
You're always there within my sight;
You show the way; You are my Light.

Lord, I love You, and I shall pray
  When the sun sets at end of day
Bringing Your Love to show the way.
Lord, I love You, come what; come may.

But Trust Me . . .

I've not been to Jerusalem;
Nor have I been to Galilee.
But trust me! I have faith in Him!
He gave His Life upon that tree.

I've not climbed to Golgotha's site;
Nor have I been to Bethlehem.
But trust me! He's my Guiding Light!
Each need I have I go to Him.

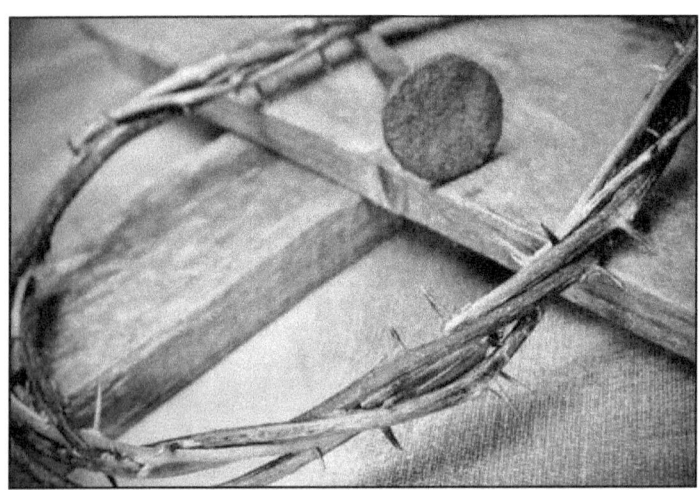

An Ever-present Friend

I love the morning stillness when
A nip is in the air;
When nightly buzzes fade away,
I greet sunrise's flair.

Shattering of the eastern skies
Produces streaks of blue;
A gentle warmth invades my world;
I offer praise to You.

The One Who makes these things occur,
Ever-present in my land;
My Truest Friend and Savior, too,
Completely in command.

And when the darkness comes to bear,
The sunset in rapture's glow!
Again, I offer praise to Him . . .
Truly a Friend to know.

I Know I Love My Jesus

I know I love my Jesus;
He's always good to me.
He picks me up if I fall down,
And He sets my spirit free.

I know I love my Jesus;
He's always at my side
Along the rocky pathways.
He cannot be denied.

I know I love my Jesus;
He considers me a gem.
He always seems to listen;
I love to talk to Him.

I know I love my Jesus;
And I'll see Him one grand day.
He is my Sun, my Guiding Star,
And He always leads the way.

My Poor Imitation

Oh Lord, grant me a brush of silk
To paint my world with broadest stroke,
Pastel tints soft as creamy milk,
Bold, bold colors to please all folk.

Grant me an easel sturdy-built
Placed near vistas of splendored hue,
Forethought to capture setting suns,
And an artist's eye tried and true.

And I shall render depictions
Of all wondrous things You have made,
Though they'll be poor imitations
And unlike Your Art they will fade.

Your Brush of Art is Masterwork
Standing the tests of time and place;
Your Colors are all Eternal:
Your Art owns the Essence of Grace.

An Endless Journey

This, the journey! Hosannas ring!
This, the journey! For Christ is King
Who came into my heart that day,
And all I had to do was pray.

This, the journey! It would appear.
Let us sing loud so all can hear
Angelic voices up from earth
Proclaiming Him from day of birth.

For a million—Nay! Trillion years
Our happiness shall bring sweet tears.
Christ shall be near to us and bless
With untold days of happiness.

Forgive My Selfishness

Dear Lord, give me one day of rest,
　Just one day that's free of pain.
And to my life please add some zest,
　So that I'd feel young again.

And one day soon I'll strut about,
　So confident in my life.
Your Praises then I'd surely tout,
　For then I'd be free of strife.

But Lord, I'm selfish. That is so;
My thoughts should center on You;
You suffered pain so I would know
　Full Grace and Salvation true.

So I'll live with my pulsing pain
　And worship You as I go;
And thank You twice and twice again
　For the gifts You do bestow.

www.ingramcontent.com/pod-product-compliance
Lightning Source LLC
Chambersburg PA
CBHW050333230426
43663CB00010B/1844